History of the Sacajawea Chapter
Olympia, Washington
Our Founding Members
& Their Legacy

By

Diane C. Whetstone

ISBN: 979-8-9937678-0-2
Printed in the United States of America

The text of this book was originally generated with the assistance of artificial intelligence and subsequently edited, rewritten, and verified by the author. All historical content, interpretations, and final composition reflect the author's original research and authorship.

Some images have been digitally restored for preservation but not enhanced or altered.

The front cover illustration depicting the women was AI-generated and edited.

All other images are either in the public domain, used with permission, or created by the author.

Published by StoneCart Books
Olympia, Washington

I dedicate this book to my incredible friends and sisters at the Sacajawea Chapter NSDAR, whose help and encouragement made this research project a reality!

And a special thanks to my daughter Mary Lou Sandler for her tremendous help with the detail on the cover graphics.

I am deeply grateful to the chapter members and friends, Diane Markham, Ann Olson, and Marilyn Rottle, for their invaluable editorial insights and tireless work in refining this book.

Table of Contents

Preface

Hello Fellow DAR Sisters and Historians,

Eight years ago, I joined my local DAR chapter. I am excited to share a project about the Sacajawea Chapter in Olympia, Washington, which will celebrate its 120th anniversary in 2025. This is the perfect time to honor the 13 women who founded the chapter in 1905.

This book is more than just dates and events. Through its pages, you will meet these founding women. Their world comes alive, and their legacy endures.

Writing this book was truly rewarding. I spent many hours reading old newspapers, examining local archives, and reviewing DAR chapter records from 1904 to 1930. It was fascinating to see how the community viewed events during that time. I also uncovered stories about Sacajawea herself, especially surrounding the 1905 centennial of the Lewis and Clark Expedition, which likely inspired the chapter's name.

Drawing on my genealogical skills, I traced the 13 founding members and learned about their parents, spouses, and children. The more I researched, the more these women became real to me, and I gained insight into their choices and dedication.

As newspaper articles, public documents, and family histories surfaced, I uncovered stories that might have otherwise been lost. I also consulted historical books to better understand the eras and communities in which they lived.

Modern research tools helped me organize timelines and connect information, but every fact was verified through primary and reliable sources. I ensured that each story is accurate, respectful, and grounded in documented history.

I hope this book is more than just a historical record. Let it inspire you and remind you of the strength of the women who came before us. Whether you are a DAR member, a historian, or simply someone who appreciates local history, I believe you will find something meaningful here.

Thank you for joining me on this heartfelt journey. It represents 120 years of dedication and love for our chapter and our country.

With warm regards,
Diane C. Whetstone
Sacajawea Chapter Registrar
DAR Volunteer Genealogist
DAR Volunteer Information Specialist
DAR Member since 2017

Figure 0.1. Chapter Graphic

Sacajawea Chapter Early History

The Sacajawea Chapter of the Daughters of the American Revolution (DAR) has a long tradition of patriotism and community involvement in Olympia, Washington. It started in the early 1900s when 13 women came together to help preserve American heritage and encourage patriotic values.

The Genesis: 1905-1909

The idea of forming a Daughters of the American Revolution (DAR) chapter in Olympia had been in the works for some time before its official formation. On Saturday, November 11, 1905, the organization was formally established at the home of Mrs. Elizabeth Lord. The primary objective of the DAR was to honor the memory and spirit of those who achieved American independence, encourage the spread of knowledge, and cherish and extend the institutions of American freedom. Membership was open to female descendants of Revolutionary patriots, with each applicant requiring endorsement by at least one national society member and approval by the general board of management.

Thirteen women from Olympia officially organized the Sacajawea Chapter of the NSDAR on November 17, 1905. The founders chose the name "Sacajawea" to honor the courageous Shoshone Indian woman who guided the Lewis and Clark Expedition to the Pacific Ocean, symbolizing a connection to American exploration and bravery. A charter was officially granted to the chapter by the National Society Daughters of the American Revolution (NSDAR) on December 5, 1906.

The 13 charter members were Mesdames Elizabeth Reynolds Lord, Sally Foster Eaton, Sue O'Bannon Porter Streets, Gertrude Wheeler Vance, Ella May Rowell Smith, Fannie Steele O'Brien, Mary A. Bryan, Lou G. Filley, Malvina Loring Hill, Helen Gordon Mills, Rio Luta Howard, Mary A McKenzie, and Miss Edith McKenzie.

The initial officers of the Sacajawea Chapter, elected on November 18, 1905, at the home of the chapter regent, Mrs. Elizabeth Lord, included:

- Elizabeth Reynolds Lord, Chapter Regent
- Sally Foster Eaton, Vice-Regent
- Sue O'Bannon Porter Streets, Secretary
- Gertrude Wheeler Vance, Corresponding Secretary
- Ella May Rowell Smith, Treasurer
- Fannie Steele O'Brien, Registrar
- Malvina Loring Hill, Historian

As reported in the DAR American Monthly Magazine dated March 1906, the chapter began under favorable conditions, showing promise as a loyal and helpful branch in the state's patriotic work. In October 1907, the Sacajawea Chapter held a meeting at the home of Mrs. M. O. Hill, with Mrs. Elizabeth Lord presiding. The meeting focused on preparing for the upcoming state assembly of the DAR, which was to be held in Tacoma in November. The chapter appointed Mrs. H. R. Hanna as its delegate to the state assembly. The meeting also discussed a local scholarship for girls and adopted a resolution to contribute to the construction of a monument at Valley Forge. Mrs. Hill and Mrs. Mills were among the guests at the meeting.

In November 1908, the chapter met at the home of Mrs. Elizabeth Lord, with Mrs. O. D. Cutts from the Mary Ball Chapter of Tacoma as a guest. The chapter made plans for its annual banquet and discussed the formation of a children's society of the

American Revolution. Mrs. Lord announced that the DAR state regent was offering prizes for the best essays by children on historical subjects. The members also discussed the chapter's historical work and their contributions to the monument at Valley Forge.

On November 16, 1909, the Sacajawea Chapter held its monthly meeting and annual luncheon at the home of Mrs. Elizabeth Lord. Mrs. Lord, the retiring regent, and Mrs. Helen Mills, the new regent, were among those present. Members from the Mary Ball Chapter of Tacoma, including Mrs. Fannie O'Brien, Mrs. Sally Eaton, Mrs. Mary Bryan, Mrs. Mary McKenzie, Mrs. Lou Filley, Mrs. Helen Mills, Miss McKenzie, and Mrs. Remington, also attended. Following the luncheon, the ladies traveled to Seattle to attend the DAR state assembly.

A Decade of Growth and Activity: The 1910s

The 1910s saw the Sacajawea Chapter continue its community involvement and patriotic endeavors. In April 1912, Mrs. Frederick T. Rice, who had recently returned from Tacoma, was scheduled to lead a discussion on the DAR work at the home of Mrs. E. G. Grimshaw.

By April 1917, the Sacajawea Chapter held an interesting meeting at the home of Mrs. John L. Bates. Mrs. N. W. O'Brien spoke on the subject of preparedness, which was a timely topic. The chapter also received a new member, Mrs. Monette Tarbell.

Community Engagement and Patriotism in the 1920s

As the 1920s dawned, the Sacajawea Chapter continued to be active in various community initiatives and patriotic programs. In February 1920, the chapter was involved in efforts to aid Americanism and to organize a movement to integrate foreign-born individuals into loyal American citizenship. The chapter participated in a joint recital with the Olympia Golf and Country Club in February 1920, featuring Mrs. Frederick A. Rice, soprano, and Miss Margaret McAvoy, harpist, both from Tacoma. The concert, held in the Olympia auditorium, attracted a good-sized audience of society people and music lovers and was a benefit for both organizations. The committee in charge of the event included Mrs. Monette Tarbell, Mrs. Elizabeth Lord, Mrs. Helen Aetzel, Mrs. Helen Mills, and Mrs. W. H. Brackett.

In March 1922, the Sacajawea Chapter held a luncheon meeting at the home of Mrs. Monette Tarbell. The principal speaker was Mrs. Walter B. Coffey, state regent of the DAR The chapter received three new members at this meeting.

The Sacajawea Chapter placed a bronze marker for the Medicine Creek Treaty grounds near Olympia. The monument was on the Brown ranch in Thurston County on McAllister Creek, about one mile west of the Pacific Highway. It notes the spot where Governor Isaac I. Stevens met with Puget Sound Indian tribes in 1854. The DAR chapter unveiled the tablet on Flag Day, June 14, 1922, with a picnic lunch and a ceremony. The marker was placed on a large fir tree thought to be the exact site of the treaty talks.

The DAR chapter had help from other groups, including the State Historical and Pioneer Societies. The ceremony had many speakers. W. P. Bonney, secretary of the State Historical Society, praised Governor Stevens. Mrs. Kate Stevens Bates, the governor's daughter, read from a book about her father's life. The tablet's inscription states, "Site of the Medicine Creek Treaty between Governor Isaac I. Stevens and the Indians of the Puget Sound basin, 1854. Marked by Sacajawea Chapter, DAR, 1922".

Though not recognized as an official historical location, the site was avoided during the creation of Interstate 5 in the 1960s. In the early 1970s, the bronze tablet placed on the original "Treaty Tree" disappeared. By 1975, the large Treaty Tree, which had been languishing for decades, was formally recognized as diseased and was dead by 1979. While the stone marker remains, the bronze plaque was later located in the Washington State Historical Society's collection.

In June 1924, the Sacajawea Chapter participated in the annual Flag Day observance. This event was organized by a committee representing various patriotic groups in Olympia, including the American Legion Auxiliary, Women's Relief Corps, and the DAR The program included a procession, a flag-raising ceremony at the Capitol, and speeches. The event was held to promote patriotic spirit and loyalty to the flag.

The Sacajawea Chapter of the Daughters of the American Revolution has consistently demonstrated its dedication to patriotic education, historical preservation, and community service throughout its existence. From its founding principles to its ongoing activities, the chapter has upheld the ideals of the DAR, ensuring that the memory and spirit of American independence are perpetuated for future generations.

THE NATIONAL SOCIETY OF THE

Daughters of the American Revolution

1776 1890

Whereas [illegible]

who are approved members of the National Society of the Daughters of the American Revolution, did, under the authorization of the National Board of Management, on the [illegible] day of November 19__, organize a Chapter of the Daughters of the American Revolution, in the City of Olympia State of Washington to be known as the Sacajawea Chapter; and Whereas the following officers of said Chapter have been selected, to wit: [illegible] as Regent, [illegible] as Vice Regent, [illegible] as Recording Secretary, [illegible] as Corresponding Secretary, [illegible] as Registrar, [illegible] as Treasurer, [illegible] as Historian.

Now, therefore, the said members and their successors and associates are hereby declared to be a regularly organized Chapter of the National Society of the Daughters of the American Revolution, to be known as the Sacajawea Chapter; and as such are entitled to all the privileges, and subject to all the limitations of the Constitution and By-Laws of the National Society.

Given under our hands and the seal of the National Society this 6th day of December 1906.

Countersigned

[illegible]

State Regent of [illegible]

[illegible]

President General.

[illegible]

V. P. G. in Charge of Organization.

[illegible]

Recording Secretary General.

Figure 0.2. Sacajawea Chapter Charter

Figure 0.3. Sacajawea statue created by artist Alice Cooper for the Lewis and Clark Expo, now located at the Washington Park, Portland, Oregon.

Honoring Sacajawea in 1905

Sacajawea, the courageous Shoshone woman who, a century prior, had guided the Lewis and Clark expedition through the vast, untamed western territories, found her heroic services publicly recognized and celebrated throughout 1905. The year was marked by a wave of tributes, from nautical voyages to monumental unveilings, all aimed at honoring the "Bird Woman".

In July, a striking new launch, aptly christened "Sacajawea," prepared for its maiden voyage down the majestic Columbia River. Built with precision and beauty by Attorney J. W. Mathews of Pullman, Washington, this five-horsepower gasoline motor craft was a "model of beauty of both line and strength," boasting a burnished brass steering wheel and a 16-inch bronze propeller. It was destined for a 500-mile cruise from Almota to Portland, Oregon, mirroring, in a modern way, the historic journey Sacajawea herself once led. Mathews, the visionary behind the boat's design and construction, captained the vessel. His crew was a diverse group of Pullmanites: E. S. Burgan, the merchant, served as purser; L. B. Miller, the jeweler, was the steward; Niel Stwart, Sr., the hardware merchant, took on the role of first mate; Will Dunean, the grocer, was the navigating officer; and Wilford Allen, a newspaper man, served as chief engineer. Adding to the colorful crew was Bill Nolan, a picturesque individual whose extensive experience as a boatman on the swift waters of the St. Lawrence earned him the title of pilot, and who promised to provide the "nautical language for the crew". The journey was anticipated to take five or six days, concluding in Portland, where the boat might find a new owner, as there were no plans to bring it back upstream by rail.

The pinnacle of the year's tributes arrived on July 6th at the Lewis and Clark Exposition in Portland, designated "Sacajawea Day". A grand bronze statue of Sacajawea and her infant child was formally unveiled amidst elaborate ceremonies attended by thousands. The statue, designed by Miss Alice Cooper of Denver, Colorado, depicted a "hardy Indian woman" with strength and grace, her papoose strapped to her back, and her hand outstretched, pointing westward, a poignant symbol of her guidance. The event was a testament to the "patient work" of the Sacajawea Statue Association, composed of public-spirited women across Oregon, Washington, Idaho, Montana, Wyoming, and Nebraska, whose objective was to elevate "one of the most heroic figures of western history out of an obscure niche into general recognition".

The day began with a parade, organized in part by the Approved Order of Red Men, marching through Portland's business district to the exposition grounds. At the ceremonies, held at 2 p.m. on Lakeview Terrace between the statues of Lewis and Clark, a huge American flag draped the monument. The invocation was delivered by Reverend Anna H. Shaw, followed by a patriotic solo, "America," sung by Charles Cutter, an Alaskan Indian. The venerable suffragist Miss Susan B. Anthony captivated the audience with her address, "Woman in Discovery," recounting Sacajawea's "patient, unfaltering deeds" in guiding the explorers when hope was nearly lost. Mrs. Abigail Scott Duniway eloquently followed with a speech titled "The Pioneer Woman." Orations were also given by Dr. H. L. Henderson, Grand Sachem of Oregon for the Independent Order of

Redmen, and T. J. Bell of Tacoma, Grand Sachem of Washington. Mrs. G. H. Pettinger read a poem dedicated to Sacajawea. Finally, Mrs. Eva Emery Dye, president of the Sacajawea association, presented the statue to the city, which Mayor Harry Lane accepted in a brief address. The statue, while remaining on its temporary pedestal during the exposition, was slated for a permanent placement in Portland, likely on the grounds of the federal building.

Beyond these grand gestures, Sacajawea's impact was recognized in other ways. The Spokane Floral Association named their club tree, a Mountain Ash, "Sacajawea". At the Lewis and Clark Exposition, Mrs. M. J. Wessells showcased "unique pictures" made from corn husks and cereals, including a life-size portrayal of Sacajawea. Furthermore, Mrs. J. A. Reed incorporated an "Indian Lullaby" dedicated to Sacajawea into her public lectures on the Lewis and Clark expedition.

While popular stories sometimes embellished her history, such as a syndication claiming the Nez Perce tribe kept her memory alive by naming a girl "Sacajawea," these were later debunked. Scholars noted that there was no "shadow of evidence" that Sacajawea ever returned to her tribe, and her story beyond an encounter with Bonneville on the lower Missouri River remained largely untraceable. However, her enduring legacy was confirmed through the discovery of her "remote descendants," including two young girls, Eunice Bazil and Fannie Myers, at the Wind River Indian school. Her son, Jean Baptiste Charbonneau, born in February 1805 at Fort Mandan, accompanied the expedition, and a grandson, Touissant Charbonneau, who died in 1905, further connected her to the generations that followed. Sacajawea, the "intrepid Indian maid," whose bravery outshone even that of the explorers she guided, finally received the enduring fame her service to the early settlement of Oregon deserved.

Figure 0.4. Souvenir Ticket - Portland Day at Lewis & Clark Expo, September 30, 1905.

A poem published in 1904 paid tribute to Sacajawea as the quiet but essential guide whose courage helped lead the Lewis and Clark Expedition across the continent. The poet portrayed her strength, endurance, and steadfastness as equal to that of the famous captains. (The full historical poem appears in Appendix A.)

Chapter 1: Mary Bryan

Mary Louise Arnold Byan
(photo not found)

Mary Louise Arnold Bryan was born on July 21, 1871, in Bedford, Iowa. She was the daughter of Nathan S. Arnold and Ellen (Goss) Arnold.

Her father, Nathan, was a grocery merchant, a farmer, and a Civil War veteran. Originally from Western New York, Nathan moved west at an early age and lived in various states in the Midwest. He accumulated a substantial amount of property while in Kansas, probably due to the Homestead Act of 1862.

In 1880, census records indicate that Mary's family was living in Kingman County, Kansas. Her family later moved to Aberdeen, Washington, in

1889. In Aberdeen, her father served multiple terms as Justice of the Peace. He also held the position of police justice for the city. He was a member of the Grand Army Post in Kingman, Kansas, and Aberdeen, Washington.

Mary's mother, Ellen, passed away in Aberdeen in 1895.

Figure 1.1. Robert Bruce Bryan

Marriage and Move to Washington

Mary married Robert Bruce Bryan on October 1, 1898 in Aberdeen, Washington. At that time, Robert worked as a teacher. He also became the Superintendent of Schools in Montesano.

In 1901, Robert was elected to a prominent role as the Superintendent of Public Instruction for

Washington State. After his election, they moved to Olympia. Mary's father moved with them.

Public Service and Activities in Olympia

Mary began working in 1902. She served as a marker for the State Board of Public Instruction. This board was responsible for teacher certification examinations. She continued this work even after her husband died.

Robert died on March 30, 1908. He passed away at their fruit ranch near Wapato, Washington and was buried in Montesano, Washington. Robert was still the State Superintendent of Public Instruction when he died.

In 1910, Mary served as a census enumerator. She worked for Thurston County.

Sacajawea Chapter, Daughters of the American Revolution (DAR)

Mary Bryan was accepted into the DAR on June 13, 1904. Her DAR National Number is 48251. She was a charter member of the Sacajawea Chapter. During the first meeting, she was appointed to the Chapter Board of Management. She also served as Chapter Regent from 1908 to 1909. According to the chapter yearbooks, she was a member of the Magazine Committee and presented during a meeting a program titled "Indian Reservations in the State of Washington".

Other Society Groups and Interests

Mary was involved in many social groups and was a founding member of some. Additionally, she hosted numerous meetings and bridge luncheons at her home.

Mary was a member of the Twentieth Century Club and the Women's Federation of Clubs. She was also active with the Ladies of the Grand Army of the Republic and the Eastern Star. She attended the First Congregational Church and once hosted the Eenati Club at her home on Water Street.

Nathan S. Arnold's Death

Mary's father passed away at her home in Olympia at the age of 83. He came to Olympia in 1901. Before that, he lived in Aberdeen for 12 years. Mary’s mother died in Aberdeen 21 years before him. Nathan was a volunteer in the Union Army during the Civil War. Injuries led to his honorable discharge. He was known for his strong character. He cared greatly for the community's welfare. Nathan was survived by his son, Charles Arnold of Aberdeen, and his daughter, Mary A. Bryan. Services were held at McClintic's chapel. His body was then taken to Aberdeen for burial.

Figure 1.2. Bryan House 1939

Building a Home in Olympia

Amidst her public service, Mary also put down roots in Olympia. In 1908, she purchased a residential lot at 15th and Water Streets. By 1910, she had built a new home on this property. The house was described as a "modern bungalow" in the Olympia Daily Recorder on April 27, 1910. It was quite spacious for its time, measuring 26 by 42 feet and featuring six rooms. The bathroom was elegantly finished with hard plaster and stained mission oak. The exterior boasted a front veranda measuring 7 by 16 feet and a side porch measuring 7 by 14 feet. Inside, it was equipped with modern conveniences like hot and cold water, gas for heat and lighting, electric lights, and even a fireplace. The construction, handled by W. H. Dodd, cost $3000. The address at the time was 1504

Water Street, and remarkably, the house, now listed as 1510 Water Street, still stands today! It's on the local register and located in the South Capitol Neighborhood National Historic District. Mary eventually sold her beloved home on Water Street in April 1920.

Political Activities

Mary was active in politics. She was an alternate delegate at the Washington State Republican Convention. This convention was held in Tacoma in 1912.

Resignation from the State School Superintendent's Office

Mary, Deputy Superintendent of Public Instruction for nearly fifteen and a half years, resigned in June 1916. Miss Lucille McKinney, her stenographer, also resigned, both directly tied to mounting conflict with Superintendent Josephine Preston.

Mary and Miss Lucille McKinney resigned because they could not support Superintendent Josephine Preston's re-election. Mary declared her resignation was voluntary, expressing she could not support Mrs. Preston in good conscience. She criticized what she saw as mismanagement, alleged mistreatment of staff, and administrative extravagance, believing Mrs. Preston was unfit for office and should not be re-elected.

Some months before her final departure in June 1916, Mary and several employees resigned after their ultimatums were unrecognized; all resignations were accepted at that time. Later, Mary apologized to Mrs. Preston and was reinstated, but ultimately resigned again in June 1916. A Columbia Twice-A-Week Chronicle article from June 21, 1916, reported these events as "Playing Politics," noting Mary's reputation as a "lawyer or agitator" suspected of undermining Mrs. Preston.

After Martha Sherwood resigned, Mary became deputy, managing the certificate department and acting as secretary to the state educational board, with Miss McKinney as stenographer. Earlier reports showed Mary remaining despite previous staff departures. The Port Townsend Daily Leader highlighted the impact of Mrs. Preston losing key staff, especially Mary, whose changing support underscored ongoing division in the administration. Mary was the twelfth assistant to leave in three and a half years. After her resignation, no original staff remained in Mrs. Preston's office.

Later Life and Travel

Mary had served the state for many years. After Mary left the Superintendent's office, her life then took new turns.

In July 1917, Mary hosted a meeting of the Daughters of the American Revolution (DAR) at her home. A paper was given on "Music of the American Indians."

Later that year, in October 1917, she took a trip. She visited her brother, Charles Arnold, who lived in Aberdeen.

In November 1917, Mary was active again with the DAR. She provided music for a chapter meeting that was held at the home of Mrs. E. J. B. Angell. Mary played piano solos titled "Marcheta" and "Spring Song."

A year later, in November 1918, she hosted another DAR meeting at her home. The program focused on music.

Mary continued to travel. In February 1919, she left for Oregon with plans to visit friends and her brother. She also intended to have minor surgery. The surgery was performed at a hospital in Portland.

By August 1921, Mary began a long journey encompassing visits friends and family. Her travels took her to St. Paul, Minnesota and along with other places in the East. She spent the winter in Florida.

In August 1922, she returned home, traveling through California. She stated her plan to live in California later on. She moved to California around 1923.

Her DAR membership was moved. It went to the Mohave Chapter in Fullerton, California. This transfer happened on February 3, 1924.

Second Marriage

On July 12, 1925, it was announced that Mary had married Dr. George Lewis Dietrich on July 2, 1925, in Los Angeles, California. Dr. Dietrich was an optometrist. This is known from census records and city directories.

Mary and Dr. Dietrich lived in Fullerton, where they stayed until 1935. In 1936, her DAR membership was listed as "inactive." They later moved to Encinitas, California.

George passed away on June 4, 1947, in Encinitas, California. His death followed a long illness. He had lived at 238 D Street, Encinitas. He was buried in Cypress View Memorial Park in Encinitas.

Final Years and Death

Mary spent her later years in California. She was a resident of San Diego County for over 50 years. This information comes from her obituary. She had lived in the county since 1915.

She was an active member of her community. She was a member and past president of the San Dieguito Women's Club. She belonged to the Encinitas Grange. Mary was also a member of the San Dieguito Methodist Church.

Mary died on May 23, 1969 in a hospital in Encinitas, California, at 97 years old. Her body was cremated.

Her life spanned a significant period of American history. From her birth in Iowa to her final years in California, Mary lived a full and active life. She was a charter member of the Sacajawea Chapter of the DAR. She held public office and was involved in many social and political activities. She was a woman dedicated to her community and country.

IN MEMORY OF
SACAJAWEA CHAPTER NSDAR
Founding Member

Mary Louise Arnold
Bryan Dietrich
1871 - 1969

Tombstone location at Fern Hill Cemetery
Aberdeen, Washington

LINEAGE BOOK

National Society of the Daughters of the American Revolution

Volume 49 - Page 119

MRS. MARY ARNOLD BRYAN. 48251

Born in Bedford, Iowa.

Wife of Robert Bruce Bryan.

Descendant of Capt. Daniel Goss.

Daughter of Nathan S. Arnold and Ellen Goss, his wife.
Granddaughter of William Goss and Abigail Fairbank, his wife.
Gr-granddaughter of Daniel Goss, Jr., and Polly Gates, his wife.
Gr-gr-granddaughter of Daniel Goss and Eunice Wilder, his wife.

Daniel Goss (1741-1809) in 1776, was captain of the 5th company, Col. Josiah Whitney's 2nd Worcester County regiment, Massachusetts militia; also in Col. James Converse's regiment, at Dobb's Ferry. He was born and died in Lancaster, Mass.

Figure 1.3

Membership Accepted by NSDAR - June 13, 1904

Chapter 2: Sally Eaton

Figure 2.0. Sally Foster Eaton

Sally Foster Eaton was born on July 18, 1866, in Cincinnati, Ohio. Her parents were Seth Cutter Foster and Julia (Resor) Foster. Sally's father, a dealer of cotton goods from Kentucky, co-founded Stearns & Foster, a mattress company in Cincinnati, Ohio, in 1846 with George Sullivan Stearns, a businessman and industrialist.

Figure 2.1. Charles Sedgwick Eaton

Marriage and Move to Olympia

On October 20, 1891, Sally married Charles Sedgwick Eaton in Hamilton, Ohio. Charles was a Harvard law graduate. He lived in Olympia, Washington, before they got married. Charles was involved in business, including real estate and banking. He was a part-owner and Vice President of West Side Mill Company. He also served on the board of the State Bank of Olympia and was a member of the Olympia City Council. He was also part of the Olympia Chamber of Commerce. Sally moved to Olympia, Washington, after their wedding. Charles suffered from lung trouble for over a year. He had sought health improvements in California and Arizona.

Figure 2.2. West Side Mill Company

Life in Olympia: Social and Civic Engagement

Sally's social life in Olympia started on January 29, 1892, when she attended a tea hosted by Mrs. General McKenny. Sally often hosted whist and euchre parties. Mrs. Elizabeth Lord was a frequent guest at these parties. While Sally's husband, Charles, handled business and politics, Sally enjoyed gardening and attending church events. She was an excellent gardener, winning prizes for her roses at annual shows. Her home was first at 516 East Bay Drive. In May 1915, she added a garage to this home. Interestingly, Sally often had trouble keeping house staff. There were constant "Help Wanted" ads in local newspapers for a housekeeper and cook.

Figure 2.3. Eaton House, 1977

Sally was actively involved in numerous social and charitable groups, frequently attending events with her husband. Her involvement first drew notice in society newspapers, including mention of the Chrysanthemum Club. As a charter member of the Olympia Outing Club, she helped create an embroidered tablecloth and napkin set for Rear Admiral Dewey, a celebrated naval hero of the Spanish-American War in 1898. Alongside Mr. Eaton, she joined the first Olympia Golf Club. She also took part in the Rector's Guild of St. John's Episcopal Church. Other group memberships included the Ladies' Relief Society and the Civic Improvement Club. Additionally, she was on the Governor's Mansion housewarming committee.

Sacajawea Chapter, Daughters of the American Revolution (DAR)

Sally Eaton was accepted into the DAR on February 7, 1905. Her DAR National Number is 50560. She served as the First Vice Regent of her chapter from 1905 to 1908. According to the chapter yearbooks she hosted some of the meetings and was a member of the Membership Committee. She resigned from the DAR on May 2, 1924. She likely joined through her sister, Julia Resor Foster (DAR #4089).

Challenges and Changes: Widowed and Motherhood

Sally faced significant challenges during her life. Her husband, Charles, passed away on July 14, 1911. He died at Neah Bay during a launch cruise. Charles had been ill with lung trouble. Sally was not with him at the time of his death. However, she traveled to be with him after he died. In November 1911, Sally took Charles's remains to Cincinnati for burial. She stayed there for the winter and returned to Olympia in May 1912 and then went back to Cincinnati in November 1913 for the winter.

Her family faced a difficult time in 1913 when a road depression occurred near her home on East Bay Avenue. The road settled by 18 inches to two feet.

This was due to a broken bulkhead along the water's edge. The roadway was sliding through.

On July 8, 1914, Sally's father died in Hamilton, Ohio. He was the head of the Stearns & Foster mattress company. He remained active in business despite his age. The following year, on October 26, 1915, her mother also passed away in Hamilton, Ohio. Sally had traveled to Cincinnati when her mother became very ill.

Sally adopted two children after her husband died. First, a daughter, Julia Sally Foster Eaton, born January 19, 1915, in Seattle. Her son, Charles Sedgwick Eaton, was born on January 16, 1917, also in Seattle. Charles, her son, died on July 18, 2002, in Newport Beach, California. He was a 1934 graduate of Olympia High School. He captained the University of Oregon tennis team. He later founded The Palisades Tennis Club. He was called "the father of tennis" in Newport Beach. He also worked as a reporter for three newspapers. These included the Eugene Register-Guard, the Honolulu Advertiser, and the Orange County Register. He was a veteran of the Washington National Guard and served in the United States Marine Corps during World War II. He was a lifelong member of Sigma Chi Fraternity.

Later Years and Philanthropic Endeavors

After becoming a widow, Sally continued her active life in Olympia, remaining deeply involved in community and social organizations. She took Red Cross First Aid classes for World War I and joined the Choral Club, the Federation of Women's Clubs, the Friday Bridge Club, the Eenati Club, the Reading Club, and the Woodbrook Hunt Club. Sally taught Sunday school and was active in both the Women's and Orthopedic Hospital Guild Auxiliaries at St. John's Episcopal Church. Her commitment extended to serving on the Salvation Army advisory board and being a charter member and treasurer of the Delphian Society. She also helped manage the Children's Farm Home at Lacey and consistently sponsored the Annual Chautauqua. This was a traveling cultural event held in a large tent that combined education and entertainment, featuring lectures by prominent figures, musical performances, and theatrical acts for the community. The American Association of University Women held a Christmas meeting at Sally's home on December 15, 1932.

Sally lived at 156 East Bay Avenue in 1913, later moving to 516 East Bay Avenue in 1915, and by 1925, she resided at 810 E Bay Drive.

Death and Legacy

Sally passed away on Monday, August 24, 1931, at St. Peter Hospital at the age of 65. She was known as one of Olympia's most respected women. Her life was largely dedicated to helping the community. She focused on the comfort and well-being of those in need. Funeral services were held on Wednesday, August 26, 1931. Her remains were at the Mills funeral parlors. She was buried at Masonic Memorial Park in Tumwater, Washington.

Preliminary actions for her will were filed on August 25, 1931. The value of her estate was not officially stated but was known to be sizable. Most of her possessions were left to her adopted daughter, Julia, 16, and son, Charles, 15. Her share in the family home in Cincinnati, Ohio, was left to her sister, Julia. Her sister was named the guardian of the children. Mrs. Gertrude Vance of Olympia was named temporary guardian until her sister could be located. Capital National Bank was appointed as trustee and administrator of the estate. A single lot in Terrace Addition was given to Katherine H. Gilshehan. Sally's will also stated that if the children did not reach adulthood, their shares would go to her sister.

IN MEMORY OF

SACAJAWEA CHAPTER NSDAR

Founding Member

Sally Foster

Eaton

1866 - 1931

Tombstone location at

Masonic Memorial Park, Tumwater, Washington

LINEAGE BOOK
National Society of the Daughters of the American Revolution
Volume 51 - Page 251

MRS. SALLY FOSTER EATON. 50560

Born in Cincinnati, Ohio.

Wife of Charles Sedgewick Eaton.
Descendant of Surgeon-General William Burnet, of New Jersey.
Daughter of Seth Cutter Foster and Julia Resor, his 3rd wife.
Granddaughter of William Resor and Mary Thew Burnet, his wife.
Gr-granddaughter of Isaac Burnet and Keturah Gordon, his wife.
Gr-gr-granddaughter of William Burnet and Gertrude Gouverneur, his wife.

William Burnet (1730-91), was a member of the Committee of Safety of Newark, where, in 1775, he established a military hospital. In 1776, he was elected to the Continental Congress and resigned to accept the position of surgeon general, Continental Army. He was a member of the original Society of the Cincinnati. He was born in Elizabeth; died in Newark, N. J.

Also No. 4025.

Figure 2.4

Membership Accepted by NSDAR - February 7, 1905

Chapter 3: Lou Filley

Figure 3.0. Louisa Jane Frazer Filley

Louisa Jane "Lou" Frazier Filley was born in September 1855 in Des Moines, Iowa. Her parents were John Frazier and Hannah (Radcliffe) Frazier. Her father was involved in farming and on December 20, 1882, purchased 160 acres as part of the Homestead Act of 1862.

On April 20, 1879, Lou married George Eno Filley in Kingman, Kansas. George was born on December 3, 1852, in St. Louis County, Missouri. His parents were Oliver Brown Filley and Mary Eno Filley. George's early life saw him attend public schools in St. Louis. He also studied at Washington University. Before moving to Kansas, he worked in the family hardware business in St. Louis. George decided to seek his fortune in the West. He arrived in Kingman, Kansas, in 1878. Like his father-in-law, George utilized the Homestead Act of 1862 to purchase 160 acres. George's was completed on June 23, 1881. Soon after, he was appointed postmaster in Kingman. This position highlights his early involvement in public service and community building.

Pioneering in Washington State

Lou and George lived in Kingman, Kansas, for about 11 years, until 1890. That year, they made a major move to the Pacific Northwest. They settled in the burgeoning Grays Harbor area of Washington State. This move was part of a larger westward migration during that era. George played a crucial role in establishing the town of Ocosta in 1890. His entrepreneurial spirit was evident in this endeavor.

Lou contribution to the new town was significant, especially in its naming. The documents indicate she was instrumental in this process. She engaged in discussions with William H. Calkins, a prominent figure from Tacoma. Their conversations led to the adoption of "Ocosta" as the town's name. This name was derived from "la costa," the Spanish term for "the coast." The addition of the letter "O" at the beginning was suggested to improve its sound, making it more distinctive and memorable. George was actively involved in the real estate business in

Ocosta. This indicates his foresight in recognizing the potential of the new coastal settlement. The Filleys' decision to move to Washington State and contribute to the founding of a new town underscores their pioneering spirit and willingness to embrace new opportunities.

Life in Olympia and Community Involvement

Lou and George time in the Grays Harbor area was relatively brief. They decided to move further north to Olympia, Washington, around 1891. This relocation brought them to the state capital. Their residence in Olympia spanned approximately two decades, leading up to George's passing in 1912.

In Olympia, George embarked on a new business venture. He opened a drug store in partnership with George Sawyer. Their establishment was located at the corner of Main and Fourth streets, a prime commercial location in the city. The drug store quickly gained popularity and prominence. It became known as one of Olympia's leading mercantile enterprises. After about 10 years, George Sawyer passed away. Despite this, the store continued to operate under its original partnership name, a testament to its established reputation. George Filley became the sole proprietor, overseeing the continued success of the company.

Figure 3.1. Location of Sawyer & Filley Drug Store

George's involvement in the community extended beyond his successful business. He was deeply committed to the civic welfare and beautification of Olympia. For approximately six years, he served on the city park board. In this capacity, he was directly involved in the development and enhancement of Priest Point Park, now named Squaxin Park. His dedication to this natural space was widely recognized. Following his death, the flag at Priest Point Park was lowered to half-staff in his honor, a public acknowledgment of his contributions. George also played a key role in the city's financial infrastructure. He helped found the Western Building & Savings Association in Olympia. The primary objectives of this association were to raise funds, provide loans to its members for real estate purposes, and accept deposits. This initiative aimed to support homeownership and local development.

Lou, while not holding public office, was also actively involved in community efforts. Her participation highlights the significant role women played in civic life during this period. A notable event in her community involvement occurred in 1899. She was part of a group of Olympia ladies who sent a thoughtful gift to Rear Admiral George Dewey. This gift was a beautiful linen set, intended as a token of appreciation. Rear Admiral Dewey sent a letter of thanks in response. His letter expressed his deep gratitude to the ladies' kindness and their elegant gift. The letter was signed simply as "Rear Admiral Dewey," emphasizing his appreciation. This exchange reflects Lou's participation in social and patriotic endeavors that connected local communities with national figures and events. A news article highlights that this was a significant gesture, as the ladies of Olympia decided to mark their respect for the Admiral in this unique way.

Society Groups

Lou was an active member of several social and civic organizations in Olympia. Her participation in these groups demonstrates her commitment to the community, extending beyond her immediate family and business. These memberships provided opportunities for social interaction, community service, and intellectual pursuits.

One of the groups she belonged to was the Women's Club of Olympia. This club was a significant part of the city's social fabric. Such clubs often played a role in cultural and educational activities for women. It provided a platform for women to gather, discuss various topics, and engage in community improvement projects.

Lou was also a member of the Olympia Golf and Country Club. This membership suggests her involvement in recreational and leisure activities. Golf clubs were popular gathering places for the affluent at the time. They offered social events and opportunities for sport.

Furthermore, she was part of the United Daughters of the Confederacy (UDC). Her membership in this organization shows a connection to Southern heritage. The UDC was primarily focused on commemorating the Confederate dead and preserving the memory of the Confederacy.

Sacajawea Chapter, Daughters of the American Revolution (DAR)

Lou Filley was accepted into the DAR on April 4, 1905. Her DAR National Number is 51641. She was a charter member of the Sacajawea Chapter. During the first meeting, she was appointed to the Chapter

Board of Management. She also served as Chapter Regent from 1915 to 1917 and as a State Board Member. She was a member of the following committees: Membership, Library, and Preservation of Historic Spots.

Later Years and Legacy

The passing of George on July 8, 1912, represented a pivotal moment in Lou's life. George was 58 years old at the time of his death. The cause of his death was listed as dropsy, a condition often associated with fluid retention, which was compounded by Bright's disease, a severe kidney ailment. He had been struggling with his health for several years leading up to his death, indicating a period of prolonged illness.

Lou and George did not have any children. This meant Lou faced her later years without direct descendants. George's funeral was held two days after his death, on July 10, at their residence in Olympia. The service was well-attended by a wide circle of friends and business associates, reflecting the high regard in which George was held in the community. As a further sign of respect, all the pharmacies in the city of Olympia closed their doors during the funeral. This gesture underscored George's prominent role as a businessman and the impact of his passing on the local commercial landscape. The Filley residence, a grand mansion located at Eleventh and Franklin streets, was considered one of the most elegant and impressive homes in Olympia. It stood as a testament to their success and standing in the community.

Following George's death, Lou, with characteristic resilience, continued to manage the Sawyer and Filley Drug Store, which was located in the Chambers Building on the prominent corner of Fourth and Main Streets. She maintained ownership of the business until 1917, demonstrating her capability and her commitment to preserving her husband's legacy. An interesting detail about the drug store was its unique offering: they produced and sold their own brand of baking powder, a testament to the era's self-sufficiency and localized commerce.

Figure 3.2. Sawyer & Filley's Baking Powder advertising tin

Later in her life, Lou made another significant move. She relocated to Seattle, Washington, where she lived for approximately 15 years. During her time in Seattle, she resided at the Wilsonian Apartments. Her move to a larger city like Seattle might have been for various reasons, possibly to be closer to other family members or to enjoy the amenities of a bigger urban center.

Lou passed away on November 13, 1943, in Seattle. Her death followed a long illness, indicating a period of declining health. Her funeral services were conducted at Forkner's Funeral Home. She was laid to rest in Olympia beside her husband, George. Her burial in Olympia signifies her enduring connection to the city where she and George had built a life and made significant contributions to the community.

Lou was survived by two of her sisters: Mrs. Ella Kinsey, who resided in Kingman, Kansas, the place where Lou and George were married, and Mrs. Sadie Hron, who lived in France. She was also survived by three nieces: Mrs. G. W. Mattson and Mrs. Vera L. Stitler, both of whom lived in Seattle, and Mrs. Ruth Schuggs of Tacoma. These surviving family members highlight the continuation of her family lineage, even in the absence of children. Lou's life spanned a period of significant change and development in the Pacific Northwest, and her story reflects the contributions of individuals in shaping new communities and participating in important social and patriotic movements. Her legacy is tied to her pioneering spirit, her community involvement, and her dedication to organizations like the DAR.

Tombstone location at Masonic Memorial Park, Tumwater, Washington

LINEAGE BOOK
National Society of the Daughters of the American Revolution
Volume 52 - Page 283

MRS. LOU J. FILLEY. 51641

Born in Des Moines, Iowa.

Wife of George Eno Filley.
Descendant of Frederick Shaver.
Daughter of John Frazier and Hannah Frazier, his wife.
Granddaughter of Samuel Frazier and Sarah Shaver, his wife.
Gr-granddaughter of Frederick Shaver and Barbara Ann Fry, his wife.

Frederick Shaver (1755-1855), enlisted, 1779, serving under Capt. Thomas Kirk and Col. Campbell, Virginia service. In 1833 he was placed on the pension roll of Greene County, Tenn. He was born in Virginia; died in Clinton County, Ind.

Figure 3.3

Membership Accepted by NSDAR - April 4, 1905

Chapter 4: Malvina Hill

Figure 4.0. Malvina Loring Hill

Malvina Loring Hill was born in June 1843 in Marseilles, Illinois. She was the beloved daughter of David Loring and Elizabeth (Nichol) Loring. Her father, a farmer by trade, frequently moved his family. He farmed lands in Illinois, relocated to Minnesota, and eventually settled in Kansas. On January 20, 1881, her father purchased 160 acres in Republic County, Kansas, as part of the Homestead Act of 1862. During Malvina's early years, America was expanding rapidly westward. Illinois had become a state just 25 years before she was born. Pioneers like her family were settling new territories. This westward movement was a defining characteristic of 19th-century America. Malvina's mother, Elizabeth, passed away in 1900. Her father, David, lived until 1909.

Marriage and Family Life

Malvina Loring and Henry Reuben Hill were married on December 12, 1867, in Mantorville, Minnesota. This was just two years after the end of the American Civil War. The nation was in a period of rebuilding and reconciliation. Henry was born in 1843 in Waterloo, Wisconsin. Like Malvina's father, Henry was also a farmer. He was also a sharp businessman. His primary focus was investing in real estate. Beyond his business interests, Henry was known for his artistic talents as an artist and a painter. He was also very involved in politics as an active member of the Democratic Party. This was a time when political allegiances were strong, especially in the wake of the Civil War.

Malvina and Henry had two children. Their first child was a son, Bradford L. Hill. Bradford was born in 1869. He chose a career in pharmacy and owned and operated the B. L. Hill Drug Company, which was also known as B. L. Hill Drug Store. He was the proprietor of Rexall Drugs in Olympia. The late 19th century saw the rise of new industries and businesses across America. Drug stores were essential community hubs. They sold medicines and other goods. Sadly, Bradford passed away in May 1912. This was eight years before his father's death.

Malvina and Henry's second child was a daughter, Miss Ida Hill. Ida was born in March 1870. She became a teacher and taught in Tacoma, Washington. Education was also growing rapidly during this period. Many women found careers as teachers. Later in life, Ida married John R. James. Like her mother, Ida was also a member of the Daughters of the American Revolution (DAR). When her mother, Malvina, passed away, Ida was living in Olympia.

Relocation to Washington

The Loring and Hill families lived in the Midwest for many years. They resided in both Minnesota and Kansas. Eventually, they made a significant move to the Pacific Northwest. The family relocated to Washington around the year 1890. This was a time of great migration to the Western states. The promise of new opportunities drew many families to the area. Washington had only become a state in 1889. This made it one of the newest states in the Union. Settling there meant being part of its early development. Upon their arrival, the Hills settled in Olympia, which became their permanent home. Henry, in particular, lived in Olympia for three decades.

Community Involvement and Social Groups

Malvina was a dedicated member of her faith. She belonged to the First Church of Christ, Scientist, in Olympia. Christian Science was a growing religious movement in the late 19th and early 20th centuries. Many communities witnessed the emergence of new churches and spiritual groups. When Malvina passed away, her funeral services were conducted by the Christian Science Society.

Her husband, Henry, was also deeply involved in the community. He was a prominent figure in several organizations and held an important position within the Masonic fraternity. The Masons were a widespread fraternal organization that emphasized self-improvement and community service. He was also a member of the Grand Army of the Republic (G.A.R.). The G.A.R. was a powerful organization of Union Civil War veterans. They played a significant role in post-Civil War American politics and society. Additionally, he was a member of the Knights of Pythias. This was another popular fraternal order. Henry served as the secretary for the Olympia Masonic Lodge No. 1. These affiliations show his commitment to civic and fraternal life in Olympia. They also highlight the importance of such societies in community building during that era.

Figure 4.1. Knights of Pythias - 1885

Sacajawea Chapter, Daughters of the American Revolution (DAR)

Malvina Hill was accepted into the DAR on April 5, 1905. Her DAR National Number is 51642. She was the chapter's first Historian from 1905 to 1908. The office of Historian was primarily focused on preserving and promoting American history, particularly as it related to the Revolutionary War and its patriots.

Pioneer Resident of Olympia

Malvina was widely recognized as a pioneer resident of Olympia. This meant she was among the early settlers who helped establish and grow the city. The family made their home at 312 Seventh Street in Olympia. They resided there around the year 1900. Her presence helped shape the city's early social fabric. As a pioneer, she witnessed and contributed to Olympia's development during a period of rapid growth for many Western cities. New infrastructure, including roads, schools, and businesses, was being constructed. She was part of a generation that laid the groundwork for modern communities.

Later Life and Death

Malvina's life came to an end at her home on East Bay Avenue in Olympia. She passed away at 8 a.m. on Tuesday, August 1, 1916. World War I had been raging in Europe for two years by this point. While America had not yet officially entered the war, the global conflict was a major backdrop to life. Malvina was a respected and well-known figure in the community. Her funeral was held on Thursday afternoon, with services beginning at 2 o'clock. They took place at the Jesse T. Mills Chapel. She was survived by her loving husband, Henry, and her devoted daughter, Miss Ida Hill. Malvina was deeply missed by her many friends in Olympia.

Her husband, Henry, continued to live in Olympia for several more years. He passed away on May 12, 1920 at St. Peter Hospital in Olympia at the age of 77. Henry had been suffering from an illness for some time. His death came in the aftermath of World War I. It was also during the time of the Spanish Flu pandemic. His funeral services were also held at the Mills Chapel. He was laid to rest at the Masonic Cemetery in Tumwater.

Legacy

Malvina left a lasting mark on Olympia. She is particularly remembered for her pivotal role in the Sacajawea Chapter, Daughters of the American Revolution. Her life story reflects the broader narrative of pioneer families. These families moved westward, settling new territories and building communities. Her contributions to Olympia, particularly her leadership in the DAR, are a significant part of her legacy. Her work ensured that the values of patriotism and historical preservation continued in her community. She lived through a remarkable period of American history, from the expansion of the frontier to the emergence of modern industries and social movements.

Tombstone location at Masonic Memorial Park, Tumwater, Washington

LINEAGE BOOK
National Society of the Daughters of the American Revolution
Volume 52 - Page 284

MRS. MALVINA LORING HILL. 51642

Born in La Salle County, Ill.

Wife of Henry A. Hill.
Descendant of Sergt. John Tilton.
Daughter of David Loring and Elizabeth Nichol, his wife.
Granddaughter of Thomas Nichol and Elizabeth Tilton, his wife.
Gr-granddaughter of John Tilton and Mariah Sutphen, his wife.
John Tilton (1756-1849), was placed on the pension roll of Richland County, Ohio, for service as private and sergeant in the New Jersey militia. He was born in New Jersey; died in Ohio.
Also No. 38464.

Figure 4.2

Membership Accepted by NSDAR - April 4, 1905

Chapter 5: Rio Howard

Figure 5.0. Rio Luta Newton Howard

Rio Luta Newton Howard lived a brief but impactful life. Born in February 1879, her early days began in Superior, Wisconsin. Her life journey ended on April 7, 1906, when she passed away in Olympia, Washington. Her death came at the young age of 27. This was a sorrowful event for her family and community. Her contributions, although brief, were remembered.

Early Life and Family Roots

Rio was the beloved daughter of James Newton and Matilda A. (Brennan) Newton. Her family had strong roots in Wisconsin. Her father played a vital role in their community, serving as Sheriff of Douglas

County and the Justice of the Peace. Sadly, James passed away early, dying of typhoid fever in 1889. Rio was only 10 years old at the time. This loss deeply affected the family. Rio's mother was born in Canada. She passed away in 1900, only a few months before Rio's wedding.

Figure 5.1. The Newton Family

Marriage

A significant event in Rio's life was her marriage to Frederick Kendall Howard on November 14, 1900. The ceremony was held at the Church of the Redeemer in Superior, Wisconsin, officiated by Bishop L. H. Nicholson of Milwaukee alongside other clergy. Rio and Frederick, serving as rector there at the time, celebrated their wedding in Douglas, Wisconsin. The event was a grand occasion amidst recent family loss.

As the only daughter in the family, Rio had three brothers. At her wedding, Charles W. Newton gave her away, stepping in for their eldest brother, Lieutenant Harry W. Newton, who was serving in the Philippines at the time. Meanwhile, Herbert W. Newton, the youngest, served as best man to Frederick. Their participation underscored the family's close ties.

Frederick K. Howard and Life in Ministry

Frederick Kendall Howard, born January 11, 1867, in Tecumseh, Michigan, dedicated himself to the ministry and became known for his long, distinguished service, which impacted many lives.

After their marriage, Frederick continued his ministry and became rector of St. John's Episcopal Church in Olympia, Washington. Their move in February 1904 marked the start of a vibrant chapter. Previously, he had served for three years at the Church of the Redeemer in Superior. In Olympia, Frederick's leadership quickly paid off the church's building debt, allowing St. John's Church to be formally consecrated on April 17, 1904. This was a proud milestone. Meanwhile, Rio became an active presence, deepening her community ties as she supported Frederick's ministry and engaged in local initiatives.

Figure 5.2. St. John's Episcopal Church - 1891

Education and Community Involvement

Rio was dedicated to her education and was a proud graduate of Nelson Dewey High School. She also completed her studies at Superior Normal. These institutions prepared her for a life of learning. Before her passing, she even worked as a substitute teacher. She filled in for Miss Alice Christie, who was ill with the grip. This showed her commitment to her community.

Upon moving to Olympia, Rio quickly became an active member of the community. She was very involved in St. John's Episcopal Church, as her faith was important to her. She took on leadership roles within the church. She was in charge of a Rector's Guild special event. This was a cooperative exchange at Van Eaton's store in the Odd Fellows building on

September 13, 1905. The purpose of the exchange was to raise money. Members sold baked goods and other items. The funds supported the Rector's Guild's activities. Her efforts helped strengthen the church community.

Untimely Passing

Rio's life was tragically cut short. She died at the age of 27 from typhoid fever. It was just one week after her second son, Frederick Rio, was born. The disease progressed rapidly, and her condition became alarming. For two days or more, her life hung in the balance. She was unconscious for nearly a day before she passed away. Her death was described as peaceful.

A premonition of her death seemed to come to Rio. She had told her family and friends that she never expected to recover. This suggests a quiet acceptance of her fate. Despite her preparedness for the end, the blow was severe. It was tough on her grief-stricken husband. He was described as all but prostrated by the loss. Her death was indeed an inexpressibly sad one and left her husband heartbroken. It also left a young son and a new baby without a mother.

In her two and a half years in Olympia, Rio became close to many people, not only in the church but throughout the community. Her passing was felt as a real loss, especially among those who shared her faith. Many in the city mourned her deeply.

Rio's Children

Rio and her husband were blessed with two sons during their brief marriage. Their first son, Clinton Newton Howard, was born on September 30, 1902. His birth took place in Superior, Wisconsin, before the family moved to Olympia. Clinton would grow up and later marry Solvejg C. Nelson on May 2, 1942, in California. He passed away on August 28, 1973, in Berlin, Vermont, and was buried there in Orange, Vermont.

Their second son, Frederick Rio Howard, was born on March 31, 1906, in Olympia, Washington. Tragically, Rio died just one week later, leaving Clinton, a 3-year-old, and Frederick Rio, a newborn. Afterward, Clinton went with his uncle and aunt, Mr. and Mrs. Clinton Howard, to their home in Bellingham, Washington. Frederick remained in Olympia, cared for by a nurse and friends. Bishop Keator later christened him in church. On December 27, 1906, Frederick was adopted by Frank Ross and Louise Tillotson Chambers Jr. His name was changed to Frederick Howard Chambers. (To find out more about Frederick's life with the Chambers family, see Chapter 14).

Legacy and Memorials

Her community cherished Rio's memory. Beautiful flowers were abundant at her funeral service. At Rev. Howard's request, only a single cluster of lilies sent by the Rector's Guild was placed on her casket. The casket itself was silver-mounted. It bore a silver plate that was inscribed with the word "Mother."

St. John's Episcopal Church received several gifts in her memory to honor her life and contributions. A family friend gave a hand-carved oak table to the church in memory of Rio. The church also received a hand-carved oak altar and reredos. Both the altar and table were made by Capus and Chamberland of Portland, Oregon, using quarter-sawn oak. The former rector donated a beautiful linen altar cloth. Two brass candlesticks were also blessed in her memory.

The Rector's Guild praised the loving memorial they completed. They even referred to Rio as the "founder of the guild." This speaks to her influential role. A choral celebration of the Holy Eucharist was held and a program of sacred music was also presented. These events were connected to the consecration of the memorial altar. St. John's parish planned to remember her death each year. They chose All Saints' Day for this remembrance. These memorials ensured that Rio's spirit and contributions would not be forgotten.

Rio was laid to rest in Nemadji Cemetery in Superior, Wisconsin, which is quite a distance from where she lived. It seems her family chose this place so she could be near her roots.

Frederick K. Howard passed away much later, on February 27, 1953, in Alameda County, California. He was laid to rest on March 5, 1953, in Oakland, California.

Sacajawea Chapter, Daughters of the American Revolution (DAR)

Rio Howard was accepted into the DAR on February 7, 1905. Her DAR National Number is 50561. She was a charter member of the Sacajawea Chapter. Her early death in April 1906 meant her time with the chapter was brief. It was just five months after the chapter's formation. Despite this short duration, her membership was meaningful. It highlighted her commitment to history. It showed her interest in preserving the past. It also demonstrated her dedication to patriotic causes. Her inclusion as a charter member underscored her active role in the community. She was part of a group dedicated to remembering and honoring American history.

Conclusion: A Lasting Impression

Rio's life was short, but she left a strong mark on her family, friends, and the Olympia community. She showed her faith by being an active member of St. John's Episcopal Church. She also gave her time to community projects like the Rector's Guild, showing how much she cared about helping others.

Building on her community involvement, her role as a charter member of the Sacajawea Chapter, Daughters of the American Revolution, speaks volumes. This position highlights her civic engagement and her pride in American history. Even in her brief association, she contributed to the founding of a historical and patriotic organization. Thus, her life, though tragically brief, was filled with purpose and dedication. She truly made a difference in the lives of those around her and remains a remembered figure in the early history of Olympia and the Sacajawea Chapter.

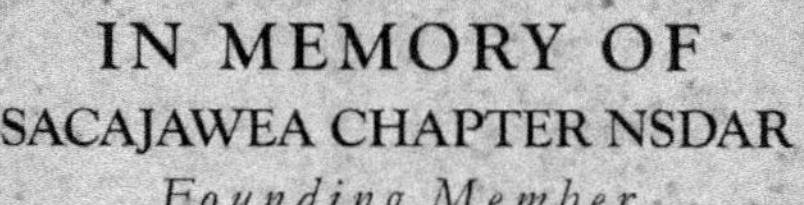

Tombstone location at Nemadji Cemetery, Superior, Wisconsin

LINEAGE BOOK
National Society of the Daughters of the American Revolution
Volume 51 - Page 251-252

MRS. RIO NEWTON HOWARD. 50561

Born in Superior, Wis.

Wife fo Frederick Kendall Howard.
Descendant of Col. Ebenezer Walbridge, Jr.
Daughter of James Newton and Matilda A. Birnnan, his wife.
Granddaughter of Henry Newton and Harriet Walbridge, his wife.
Gr-granddaughter of Henry Walbridge and Mercy Hopkins, his wife.

Gr-gr-granddaughter of Ebenezer Walbridge, Jr., and Elizabeth Stebbins, his wife.

Ebenezer Walbridge, Jr. (1738-1819), was lieutenant at the capture of Ticonderoga, Crown Point and at the siege of Quebec. He fought at Bennington and rose to the rank of colonel. He was born in Norwich, Conn.; died in Bennington, Vt.

Also No. 4667.

Figure 5.3

Membership Accepted by NSDAR - February 7, 1905

Chapter 6: Elizabeth Lord

Figure 6.0. Mary Elizabeth Reynolds Lord

Mary Elizabeth Reynolds Lord was born on November 22, 1868, in the village of Sinclairville, New York. Her parents, Henry Reynolds and Helen (Kimball) Reynolds, provided a stable and industrious upbringing. Her father was a well-respected hardware dealer in the community. His business was established in 1870, becoming a fixture in Sinclairville. Beyond his commercial ventures, Henry also served multiple terms as the supervisor of the local town, demonstrating his commitment to civic duty.

Henry's own story began on April 2, 1827, near Sinclairville, New York. The son of Abraham and Elizabeth (Smale) Reynolds, he was born eight years after their emigration from England in 1819. Growing up, Henry worked on their farm, like many of his peers. When he turned 24, he shifted from farming to the dry goods business and then established his own hardware store. His entrepreneurial spirit extended to retaining the family's original homestead and inherited farms. Later, he married Mrs. Helen (Kimball) Richmond, the daughter of Dr. Joseph E. Kimball. Their union joined two prominent regional families. Known for her intelligence and culture, Helen played an essential role in Elizabeth's early development. Elizabeth also had a brother, Elliott K. Reynolds, who would eventually reside in Tacoma, Washington

Figure 6.1. Clarence Jefferson Lord

Marriage and Family Life

Elizabeth's life changed on September 3, 1890, when she married Clarence Jefferson Lord in her hometown of Sinclairville, New York. Born in Louisville, New York, on August 16, 1863, Clarence would become a highly influential figure in Washington State. His thorough business education at Eastman's Business College prepared him for future endeavors. Clarence, the son of Bela B. and Polly Hall Lord, traced his family's local roots back to 1819, when his father came to Chautauqua County. As the visionary founder and president of the Capital National Bank in Olympia, he demonstrated remarkable financial skills and leadership. He also served as mayor of Olympia from 1902 to 1903, expanding his impact beyond banking. Their partnership was strong, rooted in shared values and a commitment to their community. Clarence's legacy endured after his passing in Olympia on February 12, 1937. He was also a member of the Olympia Masonic Lodge No. 1.

Figure 6.2. Capital National Bank, Olympia, Washington - built 1922

Elizabeth and Clarence were blessed with one daughter, Helen Elizabeth Lord, who was born on July 31, 1904, in Olympia, Washington. Helen achieved academic success, graduating from the University of Washington. On September 15, 1928, in Olympia, she married William Dennis Lucas, a banker, thus continuing the family's connection to the financial world. The couple had two children, who later lived in California. Years earlier, in August 1898, the family experienced a significant loss when Elizabeth's father, Henry Reynolds, died in London while seeking to improve his health. He had previously visited his daughter in Olympia in 1893, an experience that remained a cherished memory for Elizabeth.

Move to Olympia, Washington

Elizabeth's relocation to Olympia, Washington, in 1890 marked a new chapter in her life. This move, following her marriage, brought her to the growing capital city of Washington State. Olympia, at the turn of the 20th century, was a dynamic community, experiencing rapid growth and development. The Pacific Northwest was a region of immense opportunity during this period, attracting settlers and entrepreneurs from across the country.

A news article from August 1, 1890, noted that "Mr. C. J. Lord is about to erect a neat residence on Westside," indicating their immediate establishment in the community. Elizabeth quickly became an integral part of its social and civic fabric. Her new home provided fertile ground for her burgeoning interests in community service and historic preservation. The journey from rural New York to the Pacific Northwest was a significant one, reflecting the spirit of expansion and opportunity characteristic of the era. She embraced her new surroundings with enthusiasm, eager to contribute to the development and cultural richness of Olympia.

Civic and Social Contributions

Elizabeth distinguished herself through her extensive involvement in various public service organizations. Her dedication to community and historical preservation was evident in her affiliations. She was an active member of the United Churches, demonstrating her commitment to her faith and its role in society. Her membership in the Fortnightly Club, a women's literary and social organization, showcased her intellectual curiosity and desire for engaging discourse. Furthermore, her involvement with the Colonial Dames of the State of Washington highlighted her interest in the early history and heritage of the United States, particularly as it related to the colonial period.

Elizabeth's commitment to community was also evident in her involvement with other groups. In September 1891, she was noted as the treasurer of the newly formed Chautauqua Literary and Scientific Circle. This organization aimed to promote education and intellectual growth among women. She was also active in the Ladies' Aid Society of the Congregational Church in December 1891. Her social life included participation in events such as a whist party in January 1892 and the Ladies Musical Society in January 1892. An interesting note from February 1892 lists her among women voters on school matters, demonstrating her early engagement in local governance, even before women had full suffrage in national elections.

During the trying times of World War I, Elizabeth channeled her unrelenting energy into supporting the war effort through the Red Cross. Her leadership was recognized as she served as the chairman of the membership committee, a crucial role in mobilizing public support and resources. Her commitment extended beyond administrative duties; she actively engaged with soldiers stationed at Camp Lewis, providing comfort and assistance.

News articles from the period highlight her hands-on approach, often mentioning her tireless efforts in knitting. For instance, the Morning Olympian reported on March 18, 1918, that "Many of the garments knit by Mrs. Elizabeth Lord" were presented at a Red Cross meeting, showcasing her contribution to providing essential items for the troops. Her dedication to the Red Cross and her work with the soldiers exemplified her profound patriotism and selfless service during a critical period in history.

The Morning Olympian also noted on April 17, 1917, that Mrs. Elizabeth Lord was appointed to the Red Cross Executive Committee, further illustrating her prominent role in the organization. Another article from the Morning Olympian on September 19, 1917, mentioned that Mrs. Elizabeth Lord hosted a

Red Cross Auxiliary meeting, illustrating her ongoing involvement and leadership in local wartime efforts.

The period following World War I saw significant societal changes. The Roaring Twenties brought economic prosperity and new cultural trends. The Great Depression, beginning in 1929, brought severe financial hardship. Through these shifts, Elizabeth remained a steadfast pillar of her community, adapting her philanthropic efforts to meet evolving needs. Her husband's bank, Capital National Bank, became a branch of the Seattle National Bank of Commerce in the early 1930s, reflecting the consolidation within the banking industry during the Depression era.

Sacajawea Chapter, Daughters of the American Revolution (DAR)

Elizabeth Lord was accepted into the DAR on October 1, 1905. Her DAR National Number is 44802. She was a charter member of the Sacajawea Chapter. In 1905, Elizabeth became the first Regent of the chapter. She served as Chapter Regent 1905-1910 and Corresponding Secretary 1916-1934. She also served as a hostess for many of the chapter meetings. She was a member of the following committees: Preservation of Historic Spots, Museum and Library, Membership, Program, Americanism, and Telephone. During the meetings, she presented programs titled "Letters on Receipt of Housewives" and "The Carolinas"

Figure 6.3. Lord Mansion – built 1923

Lord Mansion

Elizabeth's philanthropy became an enduring part of her family's legacy through the Lord Mansion. Located at 211 Twenty-First Avenue in Olympia, the mansion occupies a special place in Washington's heritage. The home, commissioned by Clarence J. Lord and designed by Olympia architect Joseph Wohleb in 1923, exemplifies Spanish Colonial architecture. Its notable features include decorative friezes, carved brackets, an arched entry with Doric columns, a matching coach house, and 13 spacious rooms that reflect the grandeur of its era.

After the passing of Clarence, the family chose to honor his memory and benefit the public by gifting the mansion to the state, ensuring both its preservation and public use. Together with her daughter, Helen, she donated this remarkable home to the Washington State Historical Society. The state legislature formally accepted this generous donation in February 1939.

The Lord Mansion served as the Washington State Capitol Museum until 1993. The property and its grounds were placed under the care of the Division of Public Institutions, and the museum officially opened to the public on March 5, 1942 amid the early years of World War II, when unity and historical awareness were vital.

For decades, the museum was a popular cultural institution, despite being located in a building that wasn't originally designed for museum use. The historic structure, with its lack of climate control and other modern museum amenities, eventually became a less-than-ideal home for preserving and displaying artifacts.

In 1993, the State Capital Museum Association merged with the Washington State Historical Society, which is based in Tacoma. The Lord Mansion continued to house the museum, but its status and operations changed under the new management. Eventually, the building was deemed no longer suitable for the needs of a modern museum. The museum at the Lord Mansion closed for renovations in 2014 and never reopened to the public. The Lord Mansion and its adjacent coach house were later transferred to The Evergreen State College.

Death

Elizabeth's remarkable life came to an end on February 11, 1947. She passed away in an Olympia hospital at the age of 78. Her death occurred a decade after the passing of her beloved husband and left a void in the community that she had so diligently served. In her final years, she had been living in her home in Butler's Cove, a peaceful retreat.

A funeral service was held to honor her memory at her home in Butler's Cove, a place that had many cherished memories. The Reverend Dwight C. Smith, pastor of United Churches, conducted the service. Following the service, Elizabeth was cremated by Mills and Mills. Her final resting place is in Evergreen Cemetery in Sinclairville, New York, where she is interred alongside her husband, bringing her life's journey full circle to her birthplace.

She leaves behind a legacy of civic engagement, historic preservation, and unwavering commitment to her community and country. Her life story is a testament to the power of individual dedication in shaping the historical and cultural landscape of a region.

Tombstone location at Evergreen Cemetery, Sinclairville, New York

LINEAGE BOOK
National Society of the Daughters of the American Revolution
Volume 45 - Page 322-323

MRS. MARY ELIZABETH REYNOLDS LORD. 44802

Born in Sinclairville, New York.

Wife of Clarence J. Lord.
Descendant of Capt. Aaron Kimball.
Daughter of Henry Reynolds and Helen Kimball, his wife.
Granddaughter of Joseph Elliott Kimball and Calista Holbrook, his wife.
Gr-granddaughter of Ashael Kimball and Jerusha Elliott, his wife.

Gr-gr-granddaughter of Aaron Kimball and Mary Brooks (1737-1823) his wife, m. 1753.
Aaron Kimball (1729-1823) responded to the Lexington Alarm and commanded a company 1776 from Grafton, Worcester County, Massachusetts militia. He was born in Norwich, Conn.; died in Grafton, Mass.
Also Nos 41879, 42900.

Figure 6.4

Membership Accepted by NSDAR – October 1, 1903

Chapter 7: Mary McKenzie

Mary Ethel Woodruff McKenzie
(no photo found)

Mary Ethel Woodruff McKenzie was born on March 11, 1856 in Fort Raglan, Washington. This location was also known as the Nisqually Valley or Pierce County. She was the daughter of Samuel Nelson Woodruff and Samantha (Packwood) Woodruff.

Her mother's family, the Packwoods, were early settlers. They arrived near the Willamette River in 1844. Her father's family, the Woodruffs, had a different journey. They spent time in California during the 1849 gold rush. They returned to Washington Territory after the gold rush ended.

Mary's parents met and married in Washington Territory. This union connected two pioneering families. Mary's birth truly marked her as a child of the frontier. She grew up in a time of great change and development in the Pacific Northwest.

Marriage and Family

Mary married Peter McKenzie in 1876 in Olympia, Washington. Peter was a prominent figure. He was born on April 12, 1839, in Canada.

Peter McKenzie owned a large 500-acre farm near Mud Bay. This farm was a substantial property for its time. He was very involved in local politics and ran for county commissioner from the Third District. His involvement showed his commitment to the community. He was a member of the 1892 Republican county convention committee which was chaired by General R. G. O'Brien. This highlights Peter's connections within political circles. He was also a member of the Olympia Masonic Lodge No. 1, a fraternal organization that played an important role in the community.

Mary and Peter had eight children with one set of twins. All of them were born in Thurston County, Washington.

- Allan Donald McKenzie (1877-1951)
- Victor Ronald McKenzie (1879-1974)

- Edith Annie McKenzie (1879-1974). She married Lewis Jack Morrison. (See her biography in Chapter 9)
- Ethel Alexander McKenzie (1882-1963). She never married.
- Kenneth Roy McKenzie (1884-1923)
- Edna Anita McKenzie (1889-1963). She married Franklin E. Howard.
- Colin Clyde McKenzie (1890-1957)
- Inez E. McKenzie (1894-1972). She married Brock Medley T Payn-Sills.

The family's history is closely tied to the development of the Olympia area. Their farm and Peter's political involvement show their deep roots in the community.

Sacajawea Chapter, Daughters of the American Revolution (DAR)

Mary McKenzie was accepted into the DAR on October 3, 1905. Her DAR National Number is 53035. She was a charter member of the Sacajawea Chapter. During the first meeting, she was appointed to the Chapter Board of Management and also served as Chapter Regent from 1910 to 1911. At least three of her daughters were DAR members.

Death

Peter passed away on December 17, 1914, in Olympia, Washington. Mary passed away on

January 7, 1933, in Seattle, Washington. Her passing marked the end of a long life tied to the history of Washington. She was buried at the Masonic Memorial Park in Tumwater, Washington. This was the same cemetery where her husband, Peter, was laid to rest. Her life spanned a significant period of growth and change in the Pacific Northwest, having witnessed the transition from territory to statehood. Her contributions, particularly through her family's legacy and her involvement in the DAR, left a lasting mark.

Glengarry Golf Course (1932-1948)

After Mary's death, the family farm underwent significant changes. It became the Glengarry Golf Course. This conversion happened around 1932. The golf course operated until about 1947. This transformation marked a new chapter for the McKenzie family's land.

The Glengarry Golf Course was a major project in Olympia and was scheduled to open in early April 1932 as the city's third golf course. It had a nine-hole layout at Eld Inlet, also called Mud Bay. By opening day, most of the work was finished, and the course was built on what used to be the McKenzie farm. There was plenty of room to expand to a full 18-hole course in the future, showing the project's ambitious plans.

The name of the course was Glengarry Golf Course, though the owners indicated a "country club" title might be added later, suggesting aspirations for a more exclusive establishment. Edith McKenzie Morrison served as treasurer, while Brock Payne-Sills managed operations. The organization remained closely tied to the heirs of the Peter McKenzie estate: Miss Ethel McKenzie was named president; Ed Howard, vice president; Edith McKenzie Morrison, treasurer; and Inez Payne-Sills, secretary. This leadership structure demonstrated the family's ongoing connection to their ancestral land.

George Junor, a golf architect from Portland, Oregon, designed the course. His brother, Johnny Junor, was a well-known golf professional. The course had nine holes and measured about 3,000 yards. It was considered a flat course with many water hazards. Traps and bunkers were planned for future addition. The course was open to the public, and players would pay a greens fee. Club membership details had not yet been decided, which helped make golf available to more people.

The greens and fairways were green and smooth. Burl Sipe, an experienced worker, was in charge of their care. He had worked with George Junor on the Broadmoor course for 10 years. This expertise ensured the course was well-maintained. The nine greens were large. Putts could range from 40 to 60 feet. This made for challenging play.

The old Peter McKenzie mansion, once a showplace, was being remodeled. It was being redecorated for its new role. No locker rooms were installed initially. Future plans might include them if club memberships were offered. The remodeling included lounge rooms for men and women. There was also a dining room. Manager Payne-Sills estimated the total investment would be around $55,000. This was a substantial investment for the time.

The Glengarry Golf Course grand opening was Saturday, May 7, 1932. Greens fees would be waived for the day. This encouraged many people to visit. The Gray Harbor Transportation Company provided special round-trip rates for golfers from Olympia, making travel convenient for visitors.

The Glengarry course was laid out on historic ground. It was on the large estate of the late Peter McKenzie, a Northwest pioneer. The McKenzie heirs owned the course. Clyde McKenzie, one of the heirs, had the original idea to develop the course. He was the first president of the organization. He resigned after the first of the year.

The Glengarry clubhouse was the family home built in 1887. This retained a piece of the family's heritage. The name Glengarry had special meaning for the McKenzie family. Glengarry was the ancestral home of Peter McKenzie in Scotland. This detail connected the new venture to their family roots.

Tombstone location at Masonic Memorial Park, Tumwater, Washington

LINEAGE BOOK
National Society of the Daughters of the American Revolution
Volume 51 - Page 17

MRS. MARY E. McKENZIE. 53035

Born in Thurston County, Wash.

Wife of Peter McKenzie.
Descendant of Gedor Woodruff.
Daughter of Samuel Nelson Woodruff and Samantha Packwood, his wife.
Granddaughter of Jonathan Woodruff and Leonora Kendall, his wife.
Gr-granddaughter of Gedor Woodruff and Sarah Ingham, his 2nd wife.
Gedor Woodruff (1761-1842) enlisted at the age of seventeen, giving over three years' actual service. He was placed on the pension roll of Courtland County, N. Y., for service as private in the Connecticut Continental line. He was born in Farmington, Conn.; died in Homer, N. Y.
Also No. 21260.

Figure 7.1

Membership Accepted by NSDAR – October 3, 1905

Chapter 8: Helen Mills

Helen Gordon Mills
(photo not found)

Helen Gordon Mills was born on September 18, 1880, in Watertown, South Dakota, the daughter of Merritt James Gordon and Jennie Louise (Thompson) Gordon.

Her father, Merritt, a judge and prominent attorney, practiced law in Spokane and Tacoma before joining the Washington State Supreme Court. He arrived in Tacoma in 1883, served as assistant attorney general under Governor Eugene Semple, and was appointed superior court judge in 1893 by Governor John H. McGraw. In 1902, Governor Henry McBride appointed him to the state supreme court.

Helen's mother Jennie, was born on October 18, 1856, in Berlin, Wisconsin, and died on February 12, 1943, in Olympia, Washington, at age 86.

Education

Helen spent her early years in Washington State. She lived in Spokane and Tacoma. She completed her high school studies in 1899, graduating from Tacoma High School.

Figure 8.1. George Grant Mills

Marriage to George Grant Mills

Helen married George Grant Mills on June 25, 1902 in Spokane, Washington. George was the son of a pioneer farmer. The year before George was born his family crossed the plains from the Missouri Valley. They migrated to Tumwater, Washington, when he was a baby. George was born on May 21,

1865, in Yamhill County, Oregon. He was the second-to-last of nine children. His parents were Mr. and Mrs. George W. Mills. He spent his early childhood in Tumwater. Later, he lived at South Union. His father bought 40 acres there, and they developed a valuable farm. George received his early education in a one-room school located in South Union. He also attended Olympia Academy, which was also known as Olympia Collegiate Institute. He lived with Reverend John R. Thompson, a pioneer minister.

Residences of the Mills Family

Figure 8.2. 301 Maple Park Ave – built 1894

Figure 8.3. 2061 East Bay Drive – built 1924

Family Life and Children

Helen and George lived in Olympia after their marriage. They had five sons. They were all born in Thurston County, Washington.

- Merritt Gordon Mills (1903-1989)
- George Gordon Mills (1904-1978)
- Carroll Gordon Mills (1906-1933)
- Fleming Gordon Mills (1907-1984
- Wallace Gordon Mills (1910-1973)

George Grant Mills' Career and Civic Involvement

George had a varied and successful career, beginning as a purser on Puget Sound waters. He then worked as a clerk and later chief clerk in the U.S. Land Office, before serving as registrar from 1890 to 1894. From January 1905 to January 1909, he held the role of State Treasurer of Washington as a

Republican. Additionally, George owned Mills and Austin Hardware in Olympia.

During his career, he served two terms as Mayor of Olympia and also held the position of Superintendent of Public Safety. Residents re-elected him in December 1931, appreciating his wisdom, statesmanship, and warm, genuine friendships. As mayor, he focused on civic improvements and worked tirelessly to better the city. His long-standing activity in local politics left a mark on the community, so much so that his death came as a shock; flags were at half-staff, the city council held a special meeting, and many paid tribute to his service.

Sacajawea Chapter, Daughters of the American Revolution (DAR)

Helen Mills was accepted into the DAR on April 4, 1905. Her DAR National Number is 51643. She was a charter member of the Sacajawea Chapter. According to the archived chapter yearbooks, she hosted many of the chapter meetings and was a member of the Telephone, Magazine, and Membership Committee. She also did a presentation titled "Settlement of Rhode Island".

Civic Involvement

Helen was appointed as the first chairman of the Thurston County Red Cross, dedicating time to community service. She was involved with the Red

Cross during World War I, helping to organize local relief efforts. Her work supported soldiers and their families. She was also a member of the First Congregational Church of Olympia and was involved in its activities. She was known for her quiet nature and dedication.

George Grant Mills' Passing

Mayor George G. Mills died suddenly on January 15, 1932 at the age of 66. He died in his sleep at his home in Olympia. The cause of death was attributed to apoplexy. Helen and their son George Jr. were away on a business trip in Centralia. They returned to find him deceased. Funeral ceremonies were held at Mills Funeral Chapel. Reverend R. Franklin Hart of St. John's Episcopal Church read the service. Many city officials and friends attended the service. George was buried in Masonic Memorial Park in Tumwater, Washington. He was remembered as a devoted public servant.

Later Life and Passing

Helen passed away on February 14, 1968, in Tacoma, Washington, at the age of 87. Two sons survived her. These were Merritt Mills of Tacoma and Wallace Mills of Arlington, Virginia. Services were held at Mills and Mills' private chapel. Cremation followed the service. Helen was buried in Masonic Memorial Park in Tumwater, Washington.

Tombstone location at Masonic Memorial Park, Tumwater, Washington

LINEAGE BOOK
National Society of the Daughters of the American Revolution
Volume 52 - Page 284

MRS. HELEN GORDON MILLS. 51643

Born in Watertown, S. Dak.

Wife of George Grant Mills.
Descendant of John Conklin.
Daughter of Merritt James Gordon and Jennie Louise Thompson, his wife.
Granddaughter of Daniel Carpenter Thompson and Elmira Elizabeth McMullen, his wife.
Gr-granddaughter of Silas McMullen and Lydia Conklin, his wife.
Gr-gr-granddaughter of Jacob Conklin and Betsey McMullen, his wife.
Gr-gr-gr-granddaughter of John Conklin and Mary Parvin, his wife.
John Conklin (1758-1822), served as private and minute man in the Morris County, N. J., militia. He was born on Long Island; died in Wayne County, Pa.
Also No. 44798.

Figure 8.4

Membership Accepted by NSDAR – April 4 1905

Chapter 9: Edith Morrison

Figure 9.0. Edith Annie McKenzie Morrison

Edith Annie McKenzie Morrison was born on February 8, 1879, in Thurston County, Washington. Her parents were Peter McKenzie and Mary Ethel (Woodruff) McKenzie. (The biography of her parents and family is detailed in Chapter 7.)

Early Career and Recognition

Edith began her career teaching in Washington State public schools, mainly in Thurston County. Teaching was a highly respected profession for women at the time, reflecting their dedication to education and the community. In March 1923, she joined an Institute Program project and worked with

L. J. Morrison, who later became her husband. Working together probably brought them closer.

Edith took part in many educational and civic activities. In 1918, during World War I, she helped with the Junior Red Cross movement. As acting superintendent of Thurston County schools, she encouraged students to sell war savings stamps to support the war and get young people involved. Edith visited schools across the county to promote the program. She said the Junior Red Cross movement was one of the greatest things, believing it would teach children patriotism and self-denial. She also served on the Thurston County school board, showing her ongoing dedication to education and public service.

Sacajawea Chapter, Daughters of the American Revolution (DAR)

Edith McKenzie Morrison was accepted into the DAR on October 3, 1905. Her DAR National Number is 53036. Edith joined at the same time as her mother, Mary Ethel McKenzie. This is obvious because her DAR National Number is in sequence with her mother's, which is 53035. She was a charter member of the Sacajawea Chapter. During the first meeting, she was appointed to the Chapter Board of Management. According to the archived chapter yearbooks, she hosted several of the chapter meetings and was a member of the Membership Committee.

She also did a presentation titled "Story of the Preservation of George Washington's Home and History of the Mt. Vernon Society". Although she was a non-resident member, she remained very active within the chapter.

Marriage and Alaskan Years

Edith's personal life took a new turn when she married Lewis Jack Morrison. Their wedding took place on September 1, 1919, at the Episcopalian Church in Ketchikan, Alaska. This move to Alaska was a notable chapter in her life.

Lewis was a significant figure in his own right. He was born on December 31, 1875, in Canada. He had a varied career working as a merchant and serving in public office. Lewis was Thurston County auditor for two terms from 1907 to 1911. He also served two terms in the state legislature in 1915 and 1917. Lewis was an active member of the Republican Party. His political career shows his dedication to public service.

After getting married, the couple spent about 18 months living in Petersburg, Alaska. This time marked a unique chapter in their lives together. Life in Petersburg was quite different from what they knew in Washington. Surrounded by Alaska's natural beauty and a new way of living, they found adventure and change. While we don't know much about their daily routines, choosing to live there shows they were open to exploring and building their life as newlyweds.

Life in Oregon

After their time in Alaska, the Morrisons returned to the Pacific Northwest. They first moved to Seattle. Then, around 1924, they settled in Klamath Falls, Oregon. This move marked another shift in Edith's life.

In Klamath Falls, Edith and her sister, Ethel McKenzie, started a mercantile business called McKenzie and Morrison, described as a notion store or 5-cent and dime store. The business grew into a chain with locations in Chehalis, Toppenish, Shelton, Kelso, and Washougal, Washington, offering a wide variety of small, everyday goods. Referred to as "5c to $1 stores," these operations required a sharp retail sense and strong management skills, reflecting Edith's entrepreneurial spirit and her close partnership with Ethel.

Tragedy struck Edith's life during their time in Oregon when Lewis passed away on April 7, 1928, at age 52 in Klamath Falls. His death was a profound loss for Edith. Funeral services took place at the Mills Funeral Chapel in Olympia, bringing him back home. He was laid to rest in the Masonic Memorial Park in Tumwater, Washington.

Return to Olympia

Following Lewis's passing, Edith returned to Olympia. This move brought her back to her roots. She continued her active professional life. In 1931, she was one of the incorporators of McKenzie & Morrison, Inc. This business was established in Olympia. It had an initial capital of $30,000. Her sister Ethel was also an incorporator in this venture. This shows Edith's resilience and her continued business insight. It also highlights the ongoing partnership with her sister.

Edith played a significant role in the development of the Glengarry Golf Course as well. (See the history of the Glengarry Golf Course in Chapter 7)

Civic Engagement

In 1934, she was involved in the formation of the Thurston County Welfare Council and was elected as its treasurer. The council aimed to coordinate welfare and relief efforts in the county. Its formation came during the Great Depression. The council sought to prevent duplication of services with an aim to pool resources for maximum efficiency. This role underscores Edith's commitment to social welfare. She was actively involved in addressing community needs during a challenging time.

Later Life and Legacy

Edith touched many lives throughout her long years. She passed peacefully on August 20, 1974, in Seattle, Washington, at the age of 95. Edith was laid to rest in the Masonic Memorial Park in Tumwater, Washington, next to her beloved husband, Lewis.

Active in her community and passionate about historical preservation, Edith left a legacy that endures. As a charter member and regent of the Sacajawea Chapter DAR, she helped establish a local institution that remains significant. Her years as a teacher shaped many young minds. Showing strong business skills, she and her sister successfully pursued entrepreneurial ventures. Through the Glengarry Golf Course, Edith deepened her family's connection to the land and supported local development. Not only did she contribute to the social fabric of her community, but her dedication extended to family, education, and civic duty. The mark Edith Annie McKenzie Morrison made on Thurston County, and beyond, remains lasting.

Tombstone location at Masonic Memorial Park, Tumwater, Washington

LINEAGE BOOK
National Society of the Daughters of the American Revolution
Volume 54 - Page 17

MRS. EDITH ANNIE McKENZIE MORRISON. 53036

Born in Thurston County, Wash.

Wife of L. W. Morrison.
Descendant of Gedor Woodruff.
Daughter of Peter McKenzie and Mary Woodruff, his wife.
See No. 53035.

Figure 9.1

Membership Accepted by NSDAR – October 3, 1905

Chapter 10: Fannie O'Brien

Figure 10.0. Fannie Orlo Steele O'Brien

Fannie Orlo Steele O'Brien was born on September 2, 1856, in Oregon City, Oregon. Her father, Dr. A. H. Steele, served as an army surgeon. Her mother, Hannah (Blackler) Steele, hailed from a prominent family. Hannah, a cultured woman, traveled west from Marblehead, Massachusetts. She came to the Oregon Territory to teach and serve as a missionary.

A few years after Fannie's birth, her family relocated to The Dalles, Oregon. Soon after, they moved again to Olympia, Washington Territory. The family settled in Oregon City, Oregon, in 1860, when

Fannie was 4 years old. By 1870, at age 14, she resided in Olympia, Washington Territory.

During her younger years, the Steele home was a focal point of her life. Located at 1010 Franklin Avenue, it was a hub for social and church gatherings. The Dr. Alden H. Steele House remains standing today. It was directly across the street from the future O'Brien home.

Figure 10.1. Steele Family Home

Fannie received her education at St. Helen's Hall in Portland, an exclusive school for young women. Many of her schoolmates went on to become important figures, leading the social and civic life of the Pacific Northwest.

Marriage and Family Life

Fannie married General Rossell Galbraith O'Brien on October 23, 1878 in Thurston County, Washington. Rossell was born in November 1846 in Dublin, Ireland. At the time of their marriage, Rossell lived just two doors from Dr. Steele's home. The newly married couple initially resided in the Steele home on Franklin Street. Their own two-and-a-half-story house was built nearby. This home was located at 210 Union Avenue in Olympia. Fannie continued to live in this house until her death.

Figure 10.2. General Rossell G. O' Brien

General O'Brien had a distinguished career. He served as a Second Lieutenant during the Civil War and later rose to the rank of Brigadier General. He is credited with popularizing the custom of standing during the national anthem, "The Star-Spangled

Banner." After the war, he served as First Lieutenant of the Governor's Guards of Chicago. In 1870, he arrived in Washington Territory with Governor Edward S. Salomon. He was appointed Deputy Collector of Internal Revenue in 1871. He then served as Chief Clerk of the House of Representatives of the Legislative Assembly. He was a member of the Olympia City Council from 1886 to 1888 and served as Mayor of Olympia in 1891. Additionally, he served as Clerk of the Supreme Court of Washington. From 1880 to 1895, he was Quartermaster and Adjutant General of the Territorial Militia. He is widely recognized as the "Father" of the Washington State National Guard.

Figure 10.3. Plaque placed at Bostwick Building Tacoma, Washington

Fannie and Rossell had three children together. Florence Blackler O'Brien was born in 1879 in Washington Territory. Sadly, she died young on

March 4, 1883, in Olympia. She was laid to rest in Tumwater, Washington.

Their second daughter was Helen Kathleen O'Brien Aetzel, born on April 29, 1885, in Olympia. Helen was active in Olympia's social, civic, and church groups. She was a past Regent of the Sacajawea Chapter of the DAR. She was also a past President of the Olympia Chapter of the Daughters of the Pioneers of Washington from 1943 to 1944. Helen helped start the first Orthopedic Guild in Thurston County. She also supported the State Historical Museum, where she was a curator. For many years, Helen directed the choir at St. John's Episcopal Church.

Their son, Rossell Lloyd O'Brien, was born in May 1886 and passed away in 1912. He was a prominent student at the University of Washington where he was the captain of the Washington rowing crew.

Community Involvement and Social Groups

Fannie was a prominent social leader in Olympia for many years. She was known as one of the city's most charming hostesses. She dedicated a great deal of time to St. John's Episcopal Church, holding various offices within the church organization and remaining an active member until her health prevented further participation. She holds the distinction of being the first president of the Olympia Country Club at Butlers Cove. Fannie was also a member of the local chapter of the American Red Cross and a former member of the Ladies Relief Society.

Sacajawea Chapter, Daughters of the American Revolution (DAR)

Fannie O'Brien was accepted into the DAR on February 7, 1905. Her DAR National Number is 50532. She was a charter member of the Sacajawea Chapter. During the first meeting, she was elected as the chapter's first Registrar in 1905. Mrs. Lord recounted Fannie's dedication to the DAR noting that Fannie could have held other offices within the chapter. However, Fannie preferred to remain in the important role of Registrar. She carried out the duties of this office diligently until her passing in 1932.

According to the archived chapter yearbooks, she hosted several chapter meetings and was a member of the Museum and Library, Preservation of Historic Spots, and Membership Committees. She also did presentations titled "Indian Reservations in the State of Washington", "Historic Attempts to Annex Canada to the United States", and "Roger Williams, Founder of Rhode Island".

Later Life and Passing

Fannie's husband, General O'Brien, passed away on February 8, 1914 in Los Angeles County, California. After his death, Fannie remained in Olympia. City directories listed her as "wid Roswell" or "wid Rossell G" after 1914. She also worked as an insurance agent representing the Orient Fire Insurance Company of Hartford. Her office was located at 201 Union. Her mother, Hannah Hooper Blackler, died on February 8, 1906. Her father, Alden Hatch Steel, passed away on July 1, 1902.

Death and Burial

Fannie died on December 13, 1932, at her home, 210 Union Avenue East in Olympia, Washington at the age of 77. Her death followed a stroke she had on the previous Saturday. Before the stroke, she was in good health. She had even visited friends and neighbors earlier that day. Funeral services were held in the family home followed by burial.

Fannie was a native of Oregon and an early pioneer in the state. Her probate took place on December 19, 1932, in Thurston County, Washington. She was buried in Masonic Memorial Park in Tumwater, Washington. Her husband was buried in Mountain View Cemetery in Oakland, California.

Fannie was survived by her daughter, Mrs. Helen Aetzel, who lived in Olympia. Fannie also left behind two grandchildren, Charles A. and Miss Virginia Aetzel, who both lived in Olympia.

Centennial Park in Olympia

Centennial Park in Olympia, Washington, opened in spring 1989 to celebrate Washington State's 100th anniversary. At the center of the park stands a mature coastal redwood, known as the Daniel J. Evans Tree. This tree was planted around 1909 next to Rossell O'Brien's home, on land that once belonged to the O'Brien family. By the time the park was dedicated, the redwood was already a well-known local landmark.

Centennial Park shows Olympia's dedication to protecting mature trees and historic places. Located at Union Avenue SE and Franklin Street SE, the park still has features from when it was a residential property. Visitors can enjoy walking paths, benches, and shaded spots. The Daniel J. Evans Tree honors the former governor for his work in environmental conservation, connecting the park's history with current efforts to preserve nature.

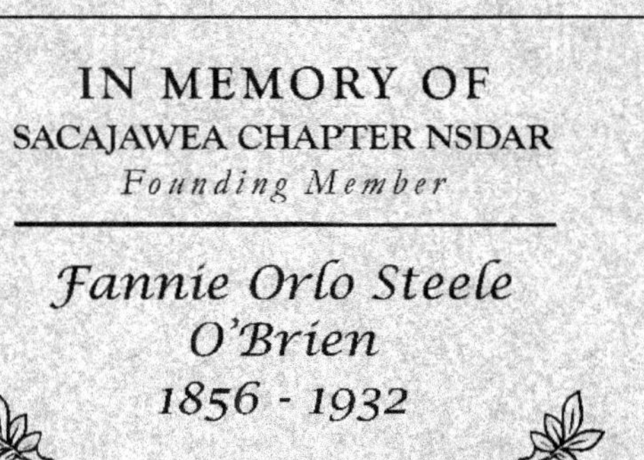

Tombstone location at Masonic Memorial Park, Tumwater, Washington

LINEAGE BOOK
National Society of the Daughters of the American Revolution
Volume 51 - Page 252

MRS. FANNY STEELE O'BRIEN. 50562

Born in Oregon City, Oregon.

Wife of Rossell Galbraith O'Brien.
Descendant of Capt. William Blackler, of Massachusetts.
Daughter of Alden Hatch Steel and Hannah Hooper Blackler, his wife.
Granddaughter of Francis Blackler and Mary Ingalls Hooper, his wife.
Gr-granddaughter of William Blackler and Rebecca Chipman, his 2nd wife.
William Blackler (1740-1818), served as captain in Col. John Glover's regiment at Long Island, and at Trenton had command of the boat in which Washington crossed the Delaware. He was lamed for life at Bemis Heights. He was born and died in Marblehead, Mass.
Also No. 18491.

Figure 10.4

Membership Accepted by NSDAR - February 7, 1905

Chapter 11: Ella Smith

Ella May Rowell Smith
(photo not found)

Ella May Rowell Smith was born on September 18, 1851, in Albany, Vermont. Her father, Joshua Converse Rowell, was born in 1819 and died on February 28, 1875, in Albany, Vermont. Her mother, Mary Fifield (Bill) Rowell, was born in 1826 and died in 1893.

Marriage and Journey West

Ella married Harry Wellington Smith on February 14, 1872, in Stowe, Vermont. Harry was born in Stowe, Vermont, in August 1850. Soon after their marriage, the couple moved to Adair, Iowa.

Their only child, Mary L. Smith, was born there on March 3, 1873. Harry worked as a store clerk in Adair.

Around 1890, the family moved to Ogdensburg, New York where Harry worked as a banker. Their daughter Mary married Jesse Blake Bridges on June 26, 1895, in Ogdensburg and soon moved to Chehalis, Washington. Harry and Ella followed their daughter to Washington. In 1901 Harry became the cashier at the Olympia National Bank.

Figure 11.1. Olympia National Bank

Harry W. Smith's Life and Career

In Olympia, Harry became a stockholder and cashier of the Olympia National Bank. He served as the bank's president until his passing. He was also a stockholder and board director of the Olympia Water Works company. Harry served as treasurer and longtime member of the Olympia Masonic Lodge No.

1. The Smith house was located next door to the Olympia Masonic Lodge No. 1.

Figure 11.2. Olympia Masonic Temple (1902)

Harry died suddenly from pneumonia in Portland, Oregon which followed an operation for gallstones. He was 61 years old at the time of his death. His body was to be cremated in Portland. His remains were probably shipped to Vermont for interment. Harry was buried in Stowe, Vermont, at Riverbank Cemetery. Ella's obituary confirms that he is buried near the old family home in Vermont.

Harry died without a will (intestate). His estate included capital stock in the Olympia National Bank worth $15,000, real estate in Thurston County, and wild timber land in Oregon. His life was insured for $4,000, and he owned other capital stocks and cash sums. The total value of his estate was estimated between $30,000 and $35,000.

Ella's Social Involvement and DAR

Ella was an active member of her community. She was a member of the First Unitarian Society Church and also belonged to the Friday Bridge Club.

Ella was a founding and charter member of three chapters of the Daughters of the American Revolution (DAR). She was admitted to the Swe-Kat-Si Chapter in Ogdensburg, New York, on June 4, 1896. She then transferred to the Robert Gray Chapter in Hoquiam, Washington, as a charter member in 1903. Finally, she transferred to the Sacajawea Chapter in Olympia, Washington, as a charter member in 1906. Her DAR national number is 14301. During the first meeting of the Sacajawea Chapter, she was elected as the first Treasurer and served from 1905 to 1908.

Widowhood and Final Residence

Harry died in 1912. After his death, Ella made her home with her sister, Mrs. C. F. David, on the Westside in Olympia. In 1913 the Olympia City Directory listed her as "wid Harry W" at 808 Main Street. By 1915 she was still in Olympia, listed as "wid Harry W" at 307 South Mill Street. This address was the home of her sister.

Death and Burial

Ella died on September 5, 1917, in Thurston County, Washington. Her death resulted from a lingering illness. She passed away on Wednesday evening at her sister's home. The funeral took place on Friday afternoon at the Jesse T. Mills undertaking chapel. Reverend C. S. Morrison officiated the service.

Ella was buried in Stowe, Vermont, at Riverbank Cemetery. Her daughter, Mrs. Mary Bridges, traveled with her body. They left Thursday evening for burial near the old family home in Vermont, where her husband is also buried.

The Bridges Family Connection

Ella's daughter, Mary L. Smith, married Jesse Blake Bridges in 1895. A key figure in Washington's legal world, Jesse B. Bridges relocated to the state in 1890 and practiced law for nearly 30 years. He served as prosecuting attorney for Grays Harbor County and as president of the Washington State Bar Association. Notably, he helped write the state's probate code, which the legislature passed in 1917. His expertise in corporate law and contributions to legislation earned him respect throughout Washington.

Building on these achievements, Jesse was appointed to the Washington State Supreme Court by

Governor Louis F. Hart in 1919. Twice re-elected, he served until his death. After a year and a half of illness, Judge Bridges died from cancer on April 14, 1927, at age 64 in Portland, Oregon.

About ten years before Mary's own death on March 8, 1952, in La Jolla, California, she was remarried to Major William J. Reed. After her passing, she was buried next to Jesse B. Bridges at the Masonic Memorial Park in Tumwater, Washington. Major Reed died in 1974 in California.

Tombstone location at Riverbank Cemetery, Stowe, Vermont

LINEAGE BOOK
National Society of the Daughters of the American Revolution
Volume 15 - Page 112-113

MRS. ELLA MAY ROWELL SMITH. 14301

Born in Vermont.

Wife of Harry Wellington Smith.

Descendant of Enoch Rowell, Sergt. Enoch Rowell, Lieut. John Johnson, Joshua Johnson and Lieut. Jacob Worthen, of New Hampshire; Col. Joseph Marsh, of Vermont.

Daughter of Joshua Converse Rowell (b. 1819) and Mary Fifield Bill, his wife (1826-93).

Granddaughter of Dr. Dyer Bill (1793-1876) and Ruth Richardson, his wife; Daniel Rowell (1786-1848) and Mercy Johnson (1791-1863), his wife (m. 1812).

Gr.-granddaughter of Eliphalet Bill and Dorothy Mason Marsh, his wife; Enoch Rowell, Jr., and Rachel Worthen, his wife (1758-1844); Joshua Johnson and Experience Barrows, his wife (1766-1850).

Gr.-gr.-granddaughter of Joseph Marsh and Dorothy Mason, his wife (m. 1750); John Johnson and Acid Johnson, his wife; Jacob Worthen and Mary Worthen, his wife; and of Enoch Rowell.

Enoch Rowell, who had fought at Louisburg, turned out in the Burgoyne campaign from Candia, and died, 1777, when he was walking home from New York.

Figure 11.3 (page 112)

Enoch Rowell, Jr., (1756-1840), served as a private and received a pension for one year's actual service in the Massachusetts Line. He died at East Plainfield.

Also No. 10125.

Joshua Johnson, (1763-1856), ran away and enlisted as midshipman and also served in the militia during the Revolution. He was born at Kittery, Maine, and was a pensioner from Albany, Vt., where he died.

John Johnson served from Greenland as sergeant in Capt. John Folsom's company, under Col. Moses Kelly, in the Rhode Island campaign, 1778. He rose to the rank of lieutenant.

Joseph Marsh, (1726-1811), served in the Provincial Congress of New York, commanded a regiment at Ticonderoga Alarm and aided in cutting the retreat of Burgoyne. He was prominent in founding the government of Vermont and was a member of the Windsor Convention, chairman of the committee to raise arms, 1777. He was elected Lieutenant Governor, 1778-79, and served in the Assembly, 1781-82.

Also No. 7452.

Jacob Worthen served from Kensington as lieutenant of the company of matross raised for the defense of Fort Washington under Capt. Titus Salter, 1777.

Figure 11.3 (page 113)

Membership Accepted by NSDAR - June 4, 1896

Chapter 12: Sue Streets

Figure 12.0. Susan O'Bannon Porter Streets

Susan O'Bannon Porter Streets was born on April 10, 1872, in Tonaconing, Maryland. She was baptized a few weeks later, on June 22, in nearby Lonaconing. Her parents were Dr. Lutellus Lindley Porter and Janet Withers Wilson Porter. Dr. Porter was well regarded in his community. He graduated from Ohio Medical College and started practicing medicine at age 21. Later, he worked as a mine physician in Roslyn, Washington, and served as a surgeon for the Northern Pacific railroad.

Early Life, Education, and Professions

Life took Sue from Maryland across the country. In 1885, when she was just 13, she lived in Des

Moines, Iowa. At this time, she was single, focusing on her early education. As she grew older, her pursuit of knowledge continued. By 1900, she was attending college in Ellensburg, Washington. She was listed as a student, diligently working on her studies. During her time in Ellensburg, she took on a professional role. For two years, she worked as a librarian at the Ellensburg Normal School. This job likely sparked her interest in library work and organization.

Her academic journey then led her to the West Coast. From 1901 to 1902, Sue was part of a special group. She joined the first co-educational class at Stanford University in Palo Alto, California. This was a notable achievement, showing her commitment to higher education. After completing her studies at Stanford, she assumed another significant role. She was appointed as the assistant state librarian in Olympia, Washington. This was an important role, reflecting her skills and dedication. She held this position until her resignation around Christmas 1903, just before her marriage in February 1904.

Sue also had experience as a private secretary working for Mr. B. F. Bush, who was the manager of the Northwestern Improvement Company in Roslyn. This showed her versatility and ability to handle different professional responsibilities. A newspaper article about her wedding also highlighted another of her talents. It mentioned that she was known for writing "strong and brilliant character sketches." These were published under a pen name, showing a creative side to her professional life. Her listed occupations truly paint a picture of an educated and active young woman. They include assistant state librarian and librarian at Ellensburg Normal School.

Figure 12.1. Ralph Raymond Streets

Marriage to Ralph R. Streets

Sue married Ralph Raymond Streets on February 2, 1904 in North Yakima, Washington. Their wedding was a local social event that was covered by the newspapers. Ralph was born on February 14, 1870, in Brockville, Ontario, Canada. He became a naturalized citizen of the United States in 1891, a major step in his life. Ralph was well-known in the lumber industry having first worked in California and gained valuable experience. Then he moved to Washington State, where his career continued to flourish.

He held prominent positions in the lumber world. He was the vice president of Pacific Tank and Pipe Company and also served as vice president of Little River Redwood Company. Ralph's entrepreneurial spirit led him to own the West Side Mill company. Later, he became vice president of another Olympia waterfront lumber company. His work often took him to various locations. His newspaper obituary noted that he managed the Redwood Company's business in Olympia, South Africa, and Australia. San Francisco served as his main headquarters for these international ventures. Ralph was a successful businessman whose work greatly influenced their family life and travels.

Figure 12.2. West Side Lumber Mill

Family Life

Sue and Ralph built a family with three daughters. Their household was vibrant and active.

Janet Nelson Streets was born on June 16, 1909, in Olympia, Washington. She lived until 1998, having a full life. Janet married Harold Jamison. Later, she married Park Reed Willis. She moved to Milwaukee, Wisconsin, at some point, as mentioned in her mother's obituary.

Susanne Streets, born on October 7, 1911, had a shorter life. She passed away in 1925 at the young age of 14. Her death, caused by pneumonia, was a tragic loss for the family.

Mary Louise Streets was born on September 20, 1912 and died on February 23, 1977. Mary pursued a career in the arts becoming a ceramic artist, showcasing her creative talent. Mary married her teacher, Edmond J. Fitzgerald who was a highly respected artist himself, part of the California Watercolor School. Edmond Fitzgerald painted murals for public projects during the 1930s. He also served as an artist during World War II, contributing his skills to the war effort. Mary and Edmond lived in Larchmont, New York, as noted in Sue's obituary.

The family often moved due to Ralph's demanding career in the lumber business. These moves likely meant new schools and new communities for the girls. Despite the changes, the family maintained their strong ties. Sue was a member of the Episcopalian church, which provided a spiritual anchor for her and her family.

Daughters of the American Revolution (DAR)

Sue Streets was a very active and devoted member of the Daughters of the American Revolution. Her connection to the DAR ran deep within her family. Her mother, Janet Withers Wilson Porter, and her two sisters, Annie M Parker and E Fay Porter, were all members. They belonged to the Narcissa Whitman Chapter in Yakima. Sue followed in their footsteps, officially joining the DAR on December 6, 1899. Her DAR National Number is 30233.

When a new chapter was being formed in Olympia, Sue played a crucial role. She transferred her membership to this new chapter, becoming one of its charter members. Sue was elected the chapter's first Recording Secretary and served from 1905 to 1908. She also served as the Chapter Regent from February 1911 to October 1913.

Later Life and Death

Sue spent her later years in different locations, reflecting her family's widespread presence. She was a former resident of Olympia, where she had been so active with the Sacajawea Chapter. In her later years, she resided in Yakima, Washington, with her sister, Annie Porter Lombard.

On July 23, 1961, Sue passed away in Newport, Rhode Island at the age of 89. She was visiting her daughter, Mary Louise Fitzgerald, at the time. Her death marked the end of a long and impactful life. A funeral service was held in Newport, Rhode Island, shortly after her passing. Following the service, her body was cremated. A graveside ceremony was held later in Yakima, Washington, allowing her family and friends there to pay their respects. She was laid to rest on September 19, 1961, in Tahoma Cemetery in Yakima, Washington. Her husband, Ralph, had passed away earlier, on May 14, 1941 in Yakima County, Washington, and is also buried in Tahoma Cemetery.

Sue left behind a legacy of family, education, and dedicated service, particularly through her significant contributions to the Daughters of the American Revolution. Her life story is a testament to the strong women who helped shape their communities and preserve American history.

Susan O'Bannon Porter
Streets
1872 - 1961

Tombstone location at Tahoma Cemetery,
Yakima, Washington

LINEAGE BOOK
National Society of the Daughters of the American Revolution
Volume 31 - Page 83

MRS. SUE O'BANNON PORTER SHEETS. 30233

Born in Tonaconing, Maryland.

Wife of Ralph R. Sheets.

Descendant of Col. Benjamin Wilson, of Virginia.

Daughter of L. Lindely Porter, M. D. and Janet Withers Wilson, his wife.

Granddaughter of Daniel Davisson Wilson and Susan O'Bannon, his wife.

Gr.-granddaughter of Benjamin Wilson and Phebe Davisson (1778-1849), his second wife, m. 1795.

Benjamin Wilson, (1747-1828), was captain of militia when the war commenced and throughout the contest was active in leading expeditions to avenge the outrages committeed by the Indians. He was born in Shenandoah; died in Harrison Co.

Also Nos. 4095, 5719, 6516, 7843, 9168, 11606, 12180, 15231, 21825, 22669, 27049.

Figure 12.3

Membership Accepted by NSDAR - November 14, 1899

Chapter 13: Gertrude Vance

Figure 13.0. Gertrude Wheeler Vance

Gertrude Wheeler Vance was born on January 21, 1867 in Milwaukee County, Wisconsin. Her parents were Colonel Junius Brutus Wheeler and Emily Truxtun (Beale) Wheeler. As with the other chapter founders Gertrude's family had a rich history.

Her mother, Emily, was born on September 7, 1832, in Washington, D.C. and died on November 16, 1880, in West Point, New York. Gertrude was only 13 when her mother passed away. Her father, Junius, was born on February 21, 1830, in Murfreesboro, North Carolina and passed away on July 15, 1886, in Lenoir, North Carolina. Gertrude was 19 when her father died. These were formative years for her.

Colonel Wheeler was a U.S. Army Colonel with an impressive military career. At age 16, he joined Major William J. Clarke's company during the Mexican War. He graduated from the United States Military Academy at West Point with high honors and became a professor of engineering there. He taught many future military leaders plus wrote several books on warfare, which helped train soldiers. He served in the Army Corps of Engineers, which handles military construction. His work was of great importance to the nation.

Sibling Relationships

Gertrude grew up in a big family with seven siblings, five sisters and two brothers. Her oldest sister, Emily Beale Wheeler, was born in 1857 in Benicia, California, and passed away in 1950 in Hickory, North Carolina. Sarah Clifton Wheeler, born in 1860 at West Point, New York, married James Goold Warren and died in 1901 in Milwaukee, Wisconsin. Mary Eliza Wheeler was born in 1863, also at West Point, and later married George Ker before her death in 1915 in Yakima, Washington. Julia Wheeler was born in 1869 in Milwaukee and died in 1943 in Hickory. Amy Wheeler, born in 1871 in Washington, DC, died in 1957 in Hickory. John Wheeler was born in 1872 but sadly died as an infant that same year at West Point. The youngest, Dr. William MacKall Wheeler, was born in 1874 at West

Point, became a US Navy physician, married Laura Forbes Denby, and died in 1913 in Washington, DC, with burial in Arlington, Virginia. The Wheeler family had strong ties to the military and faced both happy and difficult times together.

Figure 13.1. Thomas Malvern Vance

Marriage and Family Life

Gertrude married Thomas Malvern Vance on August 18, 1887 in Caldwell, North Carolina. This was shortly after her father's death. Thomas was born on September 6, 1862 in Asheville, North Carolina.

Gertrude and Thomas had no children. This was a personal choice for some couples at the time. They moved to Olympia, Washington, around 1888 which was a big move across the country. Thomas was a lawyer practicing law in North Carolina before relocating to the West. President Cleveland appointed him as a receiver of public money in Yakima, Washington, a significant federal role. In 1897, he became an Assistant Attorney General in Olympia. He held this role for two years, working for the state. He continued his career as a private attorney in the Olympia area. He was known as a "highly esteemed lawyer" in the American Blue Book, Western Washington, 1922. This exemplified his good reputation. He practiced with Frank Christensen, forming a legal partnership.

Gertrude and Thomas built two houses in Olympia. This demonstrated their commitment to the community. The first house was at 317 E 17th Avenue in 1904. Their second home, the Vance House, was built around 1925. It is located at 321 17th Ave SE. This house is in the English Revival style which was popular at the time. Gertrude owned this house until 1951, suggesting she lived there for many years after Thomas's death.

Thomas died on February 14, 1928, in Olympia, Washington. He was found in a semi-comatose state by his wife. He had suffered a paralytic stroke the previous March. This indicates a period of illness. He was 65 years old at the time of his death. His funeral was held on Thursday, February 16, 1928. He was cremated in South Tacoma after the services.

Figure 13.2. Vance House – built 1925

Sacajawea Chapter, Daughters of the American Revolution (DAR)

Gertrude Vance was accepted into the DAR on February 7, 1905. Her DAR National Number is 50563. She was a charter member of the Sacajawea Chapter. During the first meeting, she was elected as the chapter's first Corresponding Secretary and served from 1905 to 1908. She also served as Regent (1917-1919), Chaplain (1916-1917 & 1930-1932), and Board of Management (1916-1917). According to the archived chapter yearbooks, she hosted several chapter meetings and was a member of many committees, including Preservation of Historic Spots, Magazine, Program, National Defense, Correct Use of the Flag, Better Films, Radio, Press Relations, and Telephone. She also performed several presentations titled "The Beginnings of the Navy", "Traditions

Concerning Molly Pritcher", "Settlement", "History of Sacajawea Chapter", and "History of Wakefield and Mount Vernon".

Notable Events

Gertrude was involved in many social and civic events. A newspaper article from April 24, 1908, mentioned her leaving for Seattle to attend the Daughters of the American Revolution State Convention. Such conventions were important for chapter networking. Another article from March 1, 1912, stated she hosted a meeting of the DAR at her home. These show her dedication to the organization.

A Social Notes section in the local newspapers on March 27, 1919, reported "Mrs. Gertrude W. Vance" entertained the "Progressive Literary Club." This shows her involvement in other social clubs. She was also listed as a guest at various social events. For example, she was a guest at a luncheon hosted by Mrs. C. D. King on February 15, 1923. She attended a tea hosted by Mrs. F. C. Brewer on January 16, 1924. These details show her active social life in Olympia.

She was mentioned again on April 21, 1930, as a guest at a meeting of the "Olympia Women's Club." This was held at the home of Mrs. Charles W. Grinstead. This indicates her continued community involvement after her husband's death.

Death

Gertrude died on May 28, 1961 in Elma, Washington at 94 years old. She died in a nursing home, which suggests she needed care in her final years. Gertrude was cremated. Her long life spanned many historical periods. She witnessed immense changes in American society. Her contributions to her community, primarily through the DAR, left a lasting impact.

Cremated
No Tombstone Found.

LINEAGE BOOK
National Society of the Daughters of the American Revolution
Volume 51 - Page 252-253

MRS. GERTRUDE WHEELER VANCE. 50563

Born in Milwaukee, Wis.

Wife of Thomas M. Vance.
Descendant of Commodore Thomas Truxton.
Daughter of Col. J. B. Wheeler, U. S. A., and Emily Truxtun Beale, his wife.
Granddaughter of George Beale and Emily Truxton, his wife.
Gr-granddaughter of Thomas Truxton and Mary Van Drieull, his wife.

Thomas Truxton (1755-1822), commanded many privateers and made valuable captures. He was born on Long Island; died in Philadelphia.

Also Nos. 53906, 3545, 6508, 17437, 29185.

Figure 13.3

Membership Accepted by NSDAR - February 7, 1905

Chapter 14: The Tragic Story of Rio's Son

Figure 14.0. Frederick Rio Howard Chambers

This is the story of Frederick Rio Howard Chambers, a life marked by tragedy, a sensational Jazz Age scandal, and a dramatic legal fight for an inheritance.

The Olympia Infant and Adoption (Recap)

Frederick Rio Howard was born in Olympia, Washington, on March 31, 1906. His father, Frederick Kendall Howard, was a minister and rector of St. John's Episcopal Church. His mother, Rio Luta Newton Howard, was 27 at his birth and the only daughter of a former Wisconsin sheriff.

Tragedy struck almost immediately: Rio died one week later, on April 7, 1906, from typhoid fever. The infant remained in Olympia, cared for by a nurse and friends, and was christened at his father's church.

On December 27, 1906, Frederick was adopted in Oregon by Frank Ross Chambers Jr. and Louise Tillotson Chambers, becoming their adoptive son. His name was changed to Frederick Howard Chambers. (See Rio's biography in Chapter 5)

A Privileged Childhood

Frederick's adoptive family belonged to the American upper class. His father, Frank Ross Chambers Jr., born on January 8, 1874, in New York, New York, was a business executive and Vice President at the Rogers Peet Company. His grandfather, Frank Ross Chambers Sr., co-founded the multi-millionaire clothing manufacturing firm in New York. His mother, Louise Tillotson (Crandall) Chambers, born on January 28, 1878, in New Jersey, also came from a wealthy family. Louise was the daughter of James F. Crandall, a diamond dealer and manufacturer of high-class jewelry and owner of a lucrative jewelry business on Maiden Lane in New York City. Frank and Louise married on January 18, 1899, in Jersey City, New Jersey.

While Frederick's adoptive family maintained homes between San Mateo, California, and Portland, Oregon, his upbringing was further shaped by the presence of a younger adoptive sister. Marilouise Chambers was born in November 1907 in Portland, Oregon. Continuing the family's tradition of affluence and opportunity, Frederick was educated at the prestigious Thacher School in Ojai, California, and later attended the Virginia Military Institute (VMI) as a student and cadet.

In addition to their city residences, the family's connection to the countryside was established when Frank owned Featherstone Farms between 1916 and 1921. This 1500-acre dairy farm in Prince William County, Virginia, provided Frederick with memorable summers away from the city.

The Chambers Family Scandal

One day after Frank's divorce from Louise in Portland, Oregon, he married his second wife, Beatriz M. Evans, on July 21, 1923, in Tacoma, Washington. Beatriz was born on July 6, 1900, in Pennsylvania. Both stated their residences as Multnomah County, Oregon. There was a 26-year age difference between Frank and Beatriz.

The Chambers Double Tragedy

The autumn of 1924 brought a double tragedy that drew widespread public attention.

The first tragedy was the death of 17-year-old Marilouise Chambers in October 1924. Initial inquests concluded that Marilouise took her own life. News reports described her as affected by narcotics and grief, and her diary reflected her unhappiness and struggles with the drug, which was cited as evidence of suicide.

However, Marilouise's mother, Louise Chambers, publicly disputed these findings and suggested Marilouise had been murdered. The press further associated her death with personal conflict within the family, including speculation about jealousy involving her father's second wife, Beatriz Chambers.

Less than three weeks later, Frederick's adoptive father, Frank Ross Chambers Jr., died by suicide. Reports attributed his actions to grief, public scrutiny, and the effects of narcotics.

On the night of October 24, 1924, in San Mateo, California, Frank Ross Chambers Jr. took his own life. Reports noted that his burial was planned alongside his daughter.

The Dollar Son and the Estate Battle (1924–1929)

The dual suicides quickly gave way to a dramatic legal battle over Frank's substantial fortune. The estate was valued at approximately $300,000.

Frank Ross Chambers Jr.'s last will specified that the majority of the fortune, including the bulk of the $300,000 in Rogers Peet stock, would go to his mother, Kate Waller Chambers. His second wife, Mrs. Beatriz Chambers, was willed property and personal effects. Crucially, his adopted son, Frederick Howard Chambers, was explicitly left only $1 in the will.

Marilouise's mother, Louise (also Frederick's adoptive mother), immediately contested the document. The grounds for the challenge were explosive claims that Frank Ross Chambers was of "unsound mind" when the will was drawn and that it was improperly witnessed. This transformed the family tragedy into a prolonged and public "Estate Row". Frederick, as the adopted son, hired attorney C. A. Adams to fight the will.

Settlement and Aftermath

Although the estate was later declared insolvent, the legal fight did yield a result for Frederick. He received a $12,500 settlement from life insurance proceeds, which was paid outside of the main insolvent estate. The court finally closed the case in August 1929.

Relationship with Biological Father

After the suicide of Frank R. Chambers, news articles stated that Rev. Frederick K. Howard of Berkley, California, was Frank's pastor and also the father of Frederick Howard Chambers. Rev. Howard, then Chaplain of the Seamen's Church Institute of San Francisco, described himself as an old friend of the Chambers family. He was the first to reveal Frank's identity after Marilouise's suicide. It is not known if the 18-year-old Frederick Howard Chambers was aware that Rev. Howard was his biological father, but the family's connection to him indicates an ongoing relationship.

Adult Life and Career (1929–1979)

On March 6, 1929, Frederick married Alice Smoot in Frederick, Maryland; Alice was the granddaughter of Utah Senator Reed Smoot. They had a daughter, Alice Chambers, born around 1930.

Frederick began his career as a Draftsman in Washington, D.C., and worked for Stephenson's Radio Bulletin. The family later moved to Evanston, Illinois, and then North Hollywood, California. By 1950, he was working in Los Angeles as an Aircraft Engineer.

Frederick married again in November 1948 and had two more daughters, Catherine Ann Chambers and Lynn Ingram. He was later survived by his wife, Nelle Moore Chambers.

Frederick Howard Chambers died on July 10, 1979, in Fulton, Georgia, at age 73. His three daughters survived him.

Appendix A

Historical Poem:

SACAJAWEA
(The Bird-woman)

by
Bert Huffman
of Pendleton, Oregon

This poem originally appeared in the American Monthly Magazine in 1904 and reflects early efforts to honor Sacajawea's role in the Lewis and Clark Expedition. It is provided here as a historical source for reference and study.

Behind them toward the rising sun
The traversed wildernesses lay -
About them gathered - one by one,
The baffling mysteries of their way!
To Westward, yonder, peak on peak
The glittering ranges rose and fell,
Ah, but among that hundred paths
Which led aright? Could any tell?

Brave Lewis and immortal Clark!
Bold spirits of that best crusade,
You gave the waiting world the spark

That thronged the empire-paths you made!
But standing on that snowy height,
Where Westward yon wild rivers whirl,
The guide who led your hosts aright
Was that barefoot Shoshone girl!

You halted in those dim arcades -
You faltered by those baffling peaks -
You doubted in these pathless glades,
But ever, ever true she speaks!
Where lay the perilous snows of spring,
Where streams their westward course forsook,
The wildest mountain haunts to her
Were as an open picture-book!

Where'er you turned in wonderment
In that wild empire, unsurveyed,
Unerring still, she pointed West –
Unfailing, all your pathways laid!
She nodded toward the setting sun –
She raised a finger toward the sea –
The closed gates opened, one by one,
And showed your path of Destiny!

The wreath of Triumph give to her;
She led the conquering captains West;
She charted first the trails that led
The hosts across yon mountain crest!
Barefoot she toiled the forest paths,

Where now the course of empire speeds;
Can you forget, loved Western land,
The glory of her deathless deeds?

In yonder city, glory-crowned,
Where art will vie with art to keep
The memories of those heroes green –
The flush of conscious pride should leap
To see her fair memorial stand
Among the honored names that be -
Her face toward the sunset, still -
Her finger lifted toward the sea!

Beside you on Fame's pedestal,
Be hers the glorious fate to stand –
Bronzed, barefoot, yet a patron saint,
The keys of empire in her hand!
The mountain gates that closed to you
Swung open, as she led the way, -
So let her lead that hero host
When comes their glad memorial day!

Originally published in *The American Monthly Magazine* (1904); now in the public domain.

Author's Note

In preparing this book, I consulted historical newspapers, public records, genealogical resources, and archival materials. Modern digital tools were used to organize information and assist in drafting narrative sections. Every chapter was personally researched, written, and reviewed by the author to ensure historical accuracy, clarity, and consistency of voice.

This work is based on documented historical and genealogical research. While every effort has been made to verify facts through reliable sources, some details represent interpretive reconstructions drawn from public records and contemporary accounts. AI-assisted tools were used only for organizational and illustrative purposes. All final content reflects the author's original research and writing.

List of Images and Credits

Figure 0.0. *Sacajawea Chapter Founders, 1905 (AI-generated illustration)*. Digital artwork created by the author using AI image-generation software to depict 13 women in early 20th-century attire at a chapter meeting. © 2025 Diane C. Whetstone. Used with permission of the artist.

Figure 0.1. *Sacajawea Chapter graphic*. Image courtesy of the Sacajawea Chapter, Daughters of the American Revolution. Used with permission.

Figure 0.2. *Sacajawea Chapter Charter*. Image courtesy of the Sacajawea Chapter, Daughters of the American Revolution. Used with permission.

Figure 0.3. *Sacajawea statue created by artist Alice Cooper for the Lewis and Clark Expo, now located at Washington Park, Portland, Oregon*. Public domain image via Wikimedia Commons, commons.wikimedia.org

Figure 0.4. *Souvenir Ticket - Portland Day at Lewis & Clark Expo, September 30, 1905*. Courtesy of Multnomah County Library, Portland, Oregon. Public domain. gallery.multcolib.org

Figure 1.1. *Robert Bruce Bryan*. Washington State Historical Society. Public domain. washingtonhistory.org

Figure 1.2. *Bryan House, Olympia, Washington (1939)*. Thurston County Government, Assessor, Real Property Assessment Cards and Photographs, 1936–1997, Washington State Archives, Digital Archives, digitalarchives.wa.gov.

Figure 1.3. *Lineage Book*. Lineage Book, National Society of the Daughters of the American Revolution, Vol. 49 (1919), p. 119.

Figure 2.0. *Sally Foster Eaton*. Washington Secretary of State, Legacy Washington, public domain, . Digitally restored.

Figure 2.1. *Charles Sedgwick Eaton*. Public domain image from Olympia Historical Society, olympiahistory.org

Figure 2.2. *West Side Mill Company*. Historical postcard, Olympia Historical Society, public domain, olympiahistory.org

Figure 2.3. *Eaton House (1915)*. Thurston County Government, Assessor, Real Property Assessment Cards and Photographs, 1936–1997, Washington State Archives, Digital Archives, digitalarchives.wa.gov.

Figure 2.4. *Lineage Book*. Lineage Book, National Society of the Daughters of the American Revolution, Vol. 51 (1919), p. 251.

Figure 3.0. *Louise Jane "Lou" Filley*. Legacy Washington, Office of the Secretary of State, Fourth Street, Olympia. "Louise Jane 'Lou' Filley." Washington Legacymakers. Accessed April 12, 2018, sos.wa.gov

Figure 3.1. *Location of Sawyer & Filley Drug Store, Olympia*. Historical postcard, Olympia Historical Society, retrieved March 31, 2018, public domain.

Figure 3.2. *Sawyer & Filley's Baking Powder Advertising Tin*. Public domain image, likely sourced from antique auction listing, retrieved April 6, 2018.

Figure 3.3. *Lineage Book*. Lineage Book, National Society of the Daughters of the American Revolution, Vol. 52 (1919), p. 283.

Figure 4.0. *Malvina Loring Hill*. Washington Secretary of State, Legacy Washington, sos.wa.gov

Figure 4.1. *Knights of Pythias, 1885*. Courtesy of Washington State Historical Society, Thurston County History: People and Places. Verified via personal screenshot, 2018.

Figure 4.2. *Lineage Book*. Lineage Book, National Society of the Daughters of the American Revolution, Vol. 52 (1919), p. 284.

Figure 5.0. *Rio Luta Newton Howard.* Find a Grave, memorial no. 110653367, uploaded by Marlene, public domain (subject died 1906). .

Figure 5.1. *Family of Rio Matilda Newton Howard.* Find a Grave, memorial no. 110653367. Uploaded by Marlene. Accessed October 21, 2025. Public domain (subject died 1906). findagrave.com

Figure 5.2. *St.* John's Episcopal Church, Olympia, Washington (1891). Olympia Historical Society / Bigelow House Museum, public domain, olympiahistory.org.

Figure 5.3. *Lineage Book.* Lineage Book, National Society of the Daughters of the American Revolution, Vol. 52 (1919), p. 285.

Figure 6.0. *Mary Elizabeth Reynolds Lord.* Find a Grave memorial #84783468, public domain (accessed 2/20/2018).

Figure 6.1. *Clarence Jefferson Lord.* Find a Grave, memorial no. 77272720, photo ID 63429817. Accessed October 21, 2025. findagrave.com

Figure 6.2. *Capital National Bank Building, Olympia.* City of Olympia, Heritage Inventory, October 16, 1985, public domain,

.

Figure 6.3. *Lord Mansion, Thurston County Property Assessment Photograph.* Thurston County Government, Assessor. Real Property Assessment Cards and Photographs, 1936–1997. Washington State Archives, Digital Archives. Accessed April 20, 2018. digitalarchives.wa.gov

.Figure 6.4. Lineage Book. Lineage Book, National Society of the Daughters of the American Revolution, Vol. 53 (1919), p. 301.

Figure 7.1. *Lineage Book.* Lineage Book, National Society of the Daughters of the American Revolution, Vol. 51 (1919), p. 17.

Figure 8.1. *George Grant Mills.* Washington State Treasurer's Office, "Historical Gallery of Treasurers," public domain, tre.wa.gov (accessed Oct. 22, 2025).

Figure 8.2. *301 Maple Park Ave – built 1894.* Thurston County Government, Assessor, Real Property Assessment Cards and Photographs, 1936–1997, Washington State Archives, Digital Archives, digitalarchives.wa.gov (accessed Oct. 22, 2025).

Figure 8.3. *2061 East Bay Drive – built 1924.* Thurston County Government, Assessor, Real Property Assessment Cards and Photographs, 1936–1997, Washington State Archives, Digital Archives, digitalarchives.wa.gov (accessed Apr. 22, 2018).

Figure 8.4. *Lineage Book.* Lineage Book, National Society of the Daughters of the American Revolution, Vol. 51 (1919), p. 252.

Figure 9.0. *Edith Annie McKenzie Morrison.* Washington Secretary of State, Legacy Washington, "Edith Annie Morrison," public domain, sos.wa.gov (accessed Apr. 20, 2018).

Figure 9.1. *Lineage Book.* Lineage Book, National Society of the Daughters of the American Revolution, Vol. 52 (1919), p. 284.

Figure 10.0. *Fannie Orlo Steele O'Brien.* Washington Secretary of State, Legacy Washington, public domain, sos.wa.gov

Figure 10.1. *Steele Family Home, Alden Hatch Steele House (1968).* Washington State Archives, Digital Archives, digitalarchives.wa.gov

Figure 10.2. *Rossell G.* O'Brien Collection Item. Washington State Historical Society Research Collection, .

Figure 10.3. *Star-Spangled Banner Plaque, Photograph by Lynne Stallcop, used with permission.* Mary Ball DAR Chapter. Accessed October 22, 2025. maryballdar.com

Figure 10.4. *Lineage Book.* Lineage Book, National Society of the Daughters of the American Revolution, Vol. 54 (1919), p. 210.

Figure 11.1. *Olympia National Bank.* The Sunday Oregonian (Portland, OR), October 10, 1915. Public domain image via Wikimedia Commons. commons.wikimedia.org).jpg.

Figure 11.2. *Masonic Temple, Olympia, Washington (ca.* 1900–1905). Washington State Archives, State Library Photograph Collection, 1851–2024. Asahel Curtis, photographer. digitalarchives.wa.gov

Figure 11.3. *Lineage Book.* Lineage Book, National Society of the Daughters of the American Revolution, Vol. 54 (1919), p. 17.

Figure 12.0. *Susan "Sue" O'Bannon Porter Streets.* Find a Grave memorial #127928127, public domain, .

Figure 12.1. *Meet a Family: The Streets and Partlows.* Partlow, Janet. Olympia Historical Society and Bigelow House Museum, Summer 2012. Published April 27, 2012. Accessed April 12, 2018. olympiahistory.org

Figure 12.2. *Works of the West Side Mill.* Olympia Historical Society and Bigelow House Museum, public domain, olympiahistory.org

Figure 12.3. *Lineage Book.* Lineage Book, National Society of the Daughters of the American Revolution, Vol. 55 (1920), p. 144.

Figure 13.0. *Gertrude Wheeler Vance.* Sally's Family Place, sallysfamilyplace.com

Figure 13.1. *Thomas Malvern Vance.* Sally's Family Place, sallysfamilyplace.com

Figure 13.2. *Vance House Built 1925, Property Record of Thomas M.* Vance Residence. Thurston County Government, Assessor, Real Property Assessment Cards and Photographs, 1936–1997, Washington State Archives, digitalarchives.wa.gov.

Figure 13.3. *Lineage Book.* Lineage Book, National Society of the Daughters of the American Revolution, Vol. 56 (1921), p. 128.

Figure 14.0. *Frederick Howard Chambers.* Virginia Military Institute 1927 Yearbook *The Bomb* (1927), Archive.org, p. 80. Public domain.

All images in this book are either in the public domain, used with permission, or created by the author. DAR Lineage Book images were sourced from Internet Archive (archive.org). AI-generated and digitally created graphics, including cameo and memorial plaque images, were produced by the author for illustrative purposes.

Selected Bibliography and Source Notes

This book draws from a wide range of historical newspapers, public records, genealogical sources, and archival materials. The following selected bibliography lists key references and representative examples of the primary and secondary sources consulted in the preparation of this work.

A complete bibliography and image reference index are maintained by the author and available as a digital supplement at: www.sacajaweadar.org/historybook

Primary Sources

Sacajawea Chapter Early History

"Chapter of D. A. R. Here Feminine Descendants of Revolutionary Patriots Join." *Morning Olympian* (Olympia, WA), November 23, 1905, Vol. 17, no. 151, p. 1. Accessed via NewsBank: infoweb.newsbank.com

"Sacajawea Chapter." *American Monthly Magazine* 28, no. 3 (March 1906): 254. Washington, D.C.: The National Society of the Daughters of the American Revolution. Accessed via DAR Members site: services.dar.org/members/magazine_archive

"End of Oregon Trail Marked with Ceremony. Granite Boulder Is Placed by D. A. R." *Morning Olympian* (Olympia, WA), February 23, 1913, Vol. 22, no. 296, pp. 1, 4. Accessed via NewsBank: infoweb.newsbank.com

"Treaty Place to Be Marked." *Morning Olympian* (Olympia, WA), June 13, 1922, Vol. 31, no. 77, p. 4. Accessed via NewsBank: infoweb.newsbank.com

"Tablet Marks Site of Home of Governors." *Morning Olympian* (Olympia, WA), June 15, 1924, p. 2. Accessed via NewsBank: infoweb.newsbank.com

"D.A.R. Plaque to Mark Site of Old Capital." *Seattle Daily Times* (Seattle, WA), June 11, 1928, p. 32. Accessed via NewsBank: infoweb.newsbank.com

Honoring Sacajawea in 1905

"Sacajawea To Be Unvailed." *The Daily Herald* (Everett, WA), July 5, 1905, p. 6. Accessed via Newspapers.com: www.newspapers.com

"Sacajawea Veil Off." *The Daily Herald* (Everett, WA), July 6, 1905, pp. 1, 4. Accessed via Newspapers.com: www.newspapers.com

"Sacajawea (The Bird-woman)." *The News Tribune* (Tacoma, WA), January 23, 1904, p. 17. Accessed via Newspapers.com: www.newspapers.com

"Descendants of Lewis-Clark Heroine." *The News Tribune* (Tacoma, WA), August 8, 1905, p. 3. Accessed via Newspapers.com: www.newspapers.com

Chapter 1: Mary Bryan

"State Superintendent R. B. Bryan Dies in Hospital in Yakima." *Olympia Daily Recorder* (Olympia, WA), March 30, 1908, p. 1. Accessed via GenealogyBank. www.genealogybank.com.

"Mrs. Mary A. Bryan Resigns Deputy Superintendent Post." *Olympia Daily Recorder* (Olympia, WA), May 30, 1916, p. 1. Accessed via Newspapers.com. www.newspapers.com.

"Nathan S. Arnold Passes Away at Daughter's Home." *Olympia Daily Recorder* (Olympia, WA), April 6, 1920, p. 6. Accessed via Newspapers.com. www.newspapers.com.

"Mrs. Mary A. Dietrich, Longtime San Diego County Resident." *San Diego Union* (San Diego, CA), May 23, 1969, p. 15. Accessed via GenealogyBank. www.genealogybank.com.

"Dr. G. L. Dietrich, Retired Encinitas Optometrist, Dies." *San Diego Union* (San Diego, CA), June 5, 1947, p. 9. Accessed via GenealogyBank. www.genealogybank.com.

Chapter 2 – Sally Eaton

"C. S. Eaton Dies at Neah Bay on Launch Cruise." *Morning Olympian* (Olympia, WA), July 15, 1911, p. 1. Accessed via Newspapers.com. www.newspapers.com

"Much New Building Is Under Way." *Morning Olympian* (Olympia, WA), February 11, 1916, p. 1. Accessed via Newspapers.com. www.newspapers.com

"Mr Charles Sedgewick Eaton." *The Olympian* (Olympia, WA), July 25, 2002. Accessed via GenealogyBank. www.genealogybank.com

"Mrs. Charles S. Eaton Passes Away." *The Daily Olympian* (Olympia, WA), August 24, 1931, p. 1. Accessed via Newspapers.com. www.newspapers.com

"Probate of Will of Sally Foster Eaton Filed." *The Daily Olympian* (Olympia, WA), December 11, 1932, p. 3. Accessed via Newspapers.com. www.newspapers.com

Chapter 3: Lou Filley

"George E. Filley, Prominent Druggist, Passes Away." *Olympia Daily Recorder* (Olympia, WA), July 8, 1912, p. 1. Accessed via Newspapers.com. www.newspapers.com

"Ocosta-by-the-Sea: A Boomtown in Three Narratives." *Ocasta Notes* (University of Denver Thesis, quoted). Source summary used in manuscript, 2018.

"Mrs. George E. Filley Dies After Long Illness." *Seattle Daily Times* (Seattle, WA), November 15, 1943, p. 20. Accessed via GenealogyBank. www.genealogybank.com

"Mrs. Lou J. Filley, Widow of George Filley, Dies in Seattle." *The Spokesman-Review* (Spokane, WA), July 16, 1912, p. 6. Accessed via Newspapers.com. www.newspapers.com

Chapter 4: Malvina Hill

"Henry R. Hill Dead." *Morning Olympian* (Olympia, WA), May 14, 1920, p. 4. Accessed via Newspapers.com. www.newspapers.com

"Mrs. Hill, Pioneer Resident of Olympia, Dies." *The Washington Standard* (Olympia, WA), August 4, 1916, p. 8. Accessed via Newspapers.com. www.newspapers.com

"Former Resident Dies at Superior." *The Western Advocate* (Mankato, KS), August 18, 1916, p. 5. Accessed via Newspapers.com. www.newspapers.com

"Obituary of Henry R. Hill." Olympia Daily Recorder (Olympia, WA), May 13, 1920, p. 1. Accessed via Newspapers.com. www.newspapers.com

Chapter 5: Rio Howard

"Mrs. F. K. Howard Passes Away This Afternoon." *Olympia Daily Recorder* (Olympia, WA), April 7, 1906, p. 1. Accessed via Newspapers.com. www.newspapers.com

"Death of Mrs. Howard: The Church Loses an Exemplary Member and the Community a Faithful Co-Worker." *The Washington Standard* (Olympia, WA), April 13, 1906, p. 3. Accessed via Newspapers.com. www.newspapers.com

"Berkeley Funeral Services Are Held for Chaplain F. K. Howard." *Oakland Tribune* (Oakland, CA), March 4, 1953, p. 20. Accessed via Newspapers.com. www.newspapers.com

"Death Notice for Chaplain Frederick Kendall Howard." *Oakland Tribune* (Oakland, CA), March 2, 1953, p. 31. Accessed via Newspapers.com. www.newspapers.com

Chapter 6: Elizabeth Lord

"Mrs. Mary Reynolds Lord Dies at Family Home." *Daily Olympian* (Olympia, WA), February 12, 1947, p. 1. Accessed via Newspapers.com. www.newspapers.com

"Mrs. M. E. Lord, Pioneer Resident, Dies at 88." *Morning Olympian* (Olympia, WA), February 13, 1937, p. 6. Accessed via Newspapers.com. www.newspapers.com

"Women Voters Urged to Cast Ballots." *Morning Olympian* (Olympia, WA), February 26, 1892, p. 4. Accessed via Newspapers.com. www.newspapers.com

"Henry Reynolds, Father of Mrs. Lord, Prominent in Business." *Dunkirk Evening Observer* (Dunkirk, NY), August 30, 1890, p. 10. Accessed via Newspapers.com. www.newspapers.com

"Lord Mansion and Gardens." *Washington State Historical Society*. Accessed April 12, 2018. www.washingtonhistory.org

Chapter 7: Mary McKenzie

"Mud Bay Pioneer Called by Death." *The Tacoma Daily Ledger* (Tacoma, WA), January 9, 1933, p. 8. Accessed via Newspapers.com. www.newspapers.com

"Thurston Pioneer Woman Dies." *The Sunday Olympian* (Olympia, WA), January 8, 1933, p. 1. Accessed via Newspapers.com. www.newspapers.com

"Peter McKenzie, Widely Known Pioneer Dies." *Olympia Daily Recorder* (Olympia, WA), December 17, 1914, p. 1. Accessed via Newspapers.com. www.newspapers.com

"Glengarry Golf Course Planned on McKenzie Estate." *Morning Olympian* (Olympia, WA), May 5, 1932, p. 2. Accessed via Newspapers.com. www.newspapers.com

"Mary E. McKenzie, Widow of Peter McKenzie, Dies." *Morning Olympian* (Olympia, WA), January 8, 1933, p. 1. Accessed via Newspapers.com. www.newspapers.com

Chapter 8: Helen Mills

"Mayor George G. Mills Dies Suddenly." *Morning Olympian* (Olympia, WA), January 16, 1932, p. 1. Accessed via Newspapers.com. www.newspapers.com

"Obituary: Helen Gordon Mills." *Morning Olympian* (Olympia, WA), February 15, 1968, p. 12. Accessed via Newspapers.com. www.newspapers.com

Chapter 9: Edith Morrison

"Glengarry Course to Open Soon: Olympia's Third Golf Links Located at Eld's Inlet." *The Sunday Olympian* (Olympia, WA), February 28, 1932, p. 6. Accessed via Newspapers.com. www.newspapers.com

"Mrs. Edith Morrison, Former Olympia Resident, Dies." *Seattle Daily Times* (Seattle, WA), August 23, 1974, p. 59. Accessed via Newspapers.com. www.newspapers.com

"Teachers' Institute Program Booklet Mailed to Educators." *Morning Olympian* (Olympia, WA), March 8, 1905, p. 2. Accessed via Newspapers.com. www.newspapers.com

"The McKenzie & Morrison Mercantile Business Expands." *The Klamath News* (Klamath Falls, OR), November 13, 1925, p. 11. Accessed via Newspapers.com. www.newspapers.com

Chapter 10: Fannie O'Brien

"Mrs. O'Brien, Pioneer, Is Stricken." *The Daily Olympian* (Olympia, WA), December 14, 1932, p. 1. Accessed via Newspapers.com. www.newspapers.com

"Mrs. Fanny S. O'Brien, Longtime Social Leader, Dies at Her Home." *The Olympian* (Olympia, WA), December 16, 1932, p. 3. Accessed via Newspapers.com. www.newspapers.com

"General Rossell G. O'Brien Dies After Being Hurt." *Morning Olympian* (Olympia, WA), February 17, 1914, p. 1. Accessed via Newspapers.com. www.newspapers.com

"Father of National Guard Is Dead." *The Bellingham Herald* (Bellingham, WA), February 17, 1914, p. 3. Accessed via Newspapers.com. www.newspapers.com

"General Rossell O'Brien Promotes Practice of Standing for Playing of 'The Star-Spangled Banner.'" *HistoryLink.org* Essay 11102, by Duane Colt Denfeld, Ph.D. Posted November 16, 2015. www.historylink.org/File/11102

Chapter 11: Ella Smith

"Smith's Death Comes as Shock—Regret Felt Over Sudden Demise of Prominent Banker." *Morning Olympian* (Olympia, WA), May 25, 1912, p. 1. Accessed via Newspapers.com. www.newspapers.com

"Banker Harry W. Smith Dies from Pneumonia Following Operation." *Olympia Daily Recorder* (Olympia, WA), May 24, 1912, p. 1. Accessed via Newspapers.com. www.newspapers.com

"Funeral Services for Mrs. Smith Held Friday." *Morning Olympian* (Olympia, WA), September 6, 1917, p. 4. Accessed via Newspapers.com. www.newspapers.com

Chapter 12: Sue Streets

"Mrs. Sue Streets, Olympia Pioneer, Dies at 93." *The Olympian* (Olympia, WA), July 24, 1961, p. 2. Accessed via Newspapers.com. www.newspapers.com

"Funeral Services Held for Mrs. Streets." *Newport Daily News* (Newport, RI), July 26, 1961, p. 3. Accessed via Newspapers.com. www.newspapers.com

"Marriage of Miss Sue Porter to Capt. Streets." *The Tacoma Daily Ledger* (Tacoma, WA), December 24, 1903, p. 12. Accessed via Newspapers.com. www.newspapers.com

Chapter 13: Gertrude Vance

"Mrs. Gertrude Wheeler Vance Dies Suddenly." *The Seattle Daily Times* (Seattle, WA), February 15, 1928, p. 1. Accessed via Newspapers.com. www.newspapers.com

"Mrs. Vance, Civic Worker, Dies in Olympia." *The Olympian* (Olympia, WA), February 15, 1928, p. 1. Accessed via Newspapers.com. www.newspapers.com

"Mrs. Vance Remembered for Community Service." *Morning Olympian* (Olympia, WA), May 31, 1961, p. 11. Accessed via Newspapers.com. www.newspapers.com

"Marriage Announcement of Miss Gertrude Wheeler and John Vance." *The Lenoir Topic* (Lenoir, NC), August 24, 1887, p. 3. Accessed via Newspapers.com. www.newspapers.com

Chapter 14: The Tragic Story of Rio's Son

"Frederick Rio Name Change." *The Oregonian* (Portland, OR), 1906. Accessed via Newspapers.com. www.newspapers.com.

"Father Clears Mystery in Girl's Death." *The Buffalo News* (Buffalo, NY), October 10, 1924, p. 1. Accessed via Newspapers.com. www.newspapers.com.

"Jealousy Is Blamed for Girl's Death." *The Buffalo News* (Buffalo, NY), October 11, 1924, p. 1. Accessed via Newspapers.com. www.newspapers.com.

"Grandfather Bares Past in Girl's Death." *The Buffalo News* (Buffalo, NY), October 13, 1924, p. 1. Accessed via Newspapers.com. www.newspapers.com.

"Mother Denies Girl Suicide Death Theory." *The Buffalo News* (Buffalo, NY), October 14, 1924, p. 1. Accessed via Newspapers.com. www.newspapers.com.

"Police Sift Mystery Suicides of Father and Chambers Girl." *The Buffalo News* (Buffalo, NY), October 25, 1924, p. 1. Accessed via Newspapers.com. www.newspapers.com.

"Suicide Path His Daughter Trod Taken by Father." *The Buffalo News* (Buffalo, NY), October 25, 1924, p. 1. Accessed via Newspapers.com. www.newspapers.com.

"Adopted Son to Contest Document." *Alameda Times Star* (Alameda, CA), November 28, 1924, p. 1. Accessed via Newspapers.com. www.newspapers.com.

"Rich Suicide's $300,000 Will Is Contested." *Alameda Times Star* (Alameda, CA), November 28, 1924, p. 1. Accessed via Newspapers.com. www.newspapers.com.

"Frederic H. Chambers Obituary." *Redwood City Tribune* (Redwood City, CA), July 11, 1979. Accessed via Newspapers.com. www.newspapers.com.

Secondary and Reference Works

All genealogical records and historical datasets referenced in this book were accessed from Ancestry.com and FamilySearch.org, August 2025.

"United States Federal Census, 1850–1950." *Ancestry.com* and *FamilySearch.org* databases and images.

"California, County Birth, Marriage, and Death Records, 1849–1980." *Ancestry.com* and *FamilySearch.org* databases and images.

"Daughters of the American Revolution Lineage Books (152 Vols.)." *Ancestry.com* and *FamilySearch.org* databases.

"North America, Family Histories, 1500–2000." *Ancestry.com* and *FamilySearch.org* databases.

"U.S. City Directories, 1822–1995." *Ancestry.com* and *FamilySearch.org* databases and images.

"U.S. Civil War Pension Index: General Index to Pension Files, 1861–1934." *Ancestry.com* and *FamilySearch.org*databases.

"U.S. Find A Grave Index, 1600s–Current." *Ancestry.com* and *FamilySearch.org* databases.

"Washington State and Territorial Censuses, 1857–1892." *Ancestry.com* and *FamilySearch.org* databases and images.

"Washington, Wills and Probate Records, 1851–1970." *Ancestry.com* and *FamilySearch.org* databases and images.

"Washington, Death Records, 1883–1960." *Ancestry.com* and *FamilySearch.org* databases.

"U.S. Presbyterian Church Records, 1701–1970." *Ancestry.com* and *FamilySearch.org* databases.

Image and Illustration Credits

All images in this book are either in the public domain, used with permission, or created by the author. Archival photographs were located through the Washington State Digital Archives, the Library of Congress, and the author's private collection.

A full list of figure credits and image permissions accompanies the complete bibliography online.

Note to Readers

To keep this printed volume concise, only a representative selection of citations appears here. For researchers and readers interested in original newspaper scans, image archives, and source provenance, please refer to the author's supplemental materials at: www.sacajaweadar.org/historybook

About the Author

Diane C. Whetstone started working as a computer programmer in 1977 and continued in the field until she retired in 2015. During that time, she and her husband, Donnie Whetstone, also ran a fitness center for over 10 years, reflecting her dedication to health and fitness.

Diane has been interested in genealogical research since 1980, carefully exploring her family history. She joined the Sacajawea Chapter of the Daughters of the American Revolution in 2017 and has served in several roles, including Volunteer Information Specialist, Lineage Research Team member, Treasurer, and Registrar.

Born and raised in Washington State, Diane continues to bring her energy and dedication to genealogy, history, and community service, just as she did throughout her career and personal life.

Learn More or Join Us

If you would like to learn more about the Sacajawea Chapter, NSDAR, or are interested in becoming a member, we welcome your inquiry.

Sacajawea Chapter, NSDAR
Olympia, Washington

Website: www.sacajaweadar.org
Facebook: www.facebook.com/sacajaweadar

To learn more about the **National Society Daughters of the American Revolution (NSDAR)** and its mission to promote historic preservation, education, and patriotism, visit

www.dar.org

Membership in the DAR honors your heritage and helps preserve the legacy of those who shaped our nation.

www.ingramcontent.com/pod-product-compliance
Lightning Source LLC
Chambersburg PA
CBHW060422130626
46555CB00005B/2182
9798993767802